Francis, Austin.

Smart squash

Smart Squash

Books by Austin Francis

SMART SQUASH
CATSKILL FLYTIER
(Harry Darbee with Mac Francis)

Smart Squash

Using Your Head to Win

**by
Austin Francis**

*Introduction by
Victor Niederhoffer*

*Illustrations by
Michael Witte*

J. B. Lippincott Company / Philadelphia and New York

Copyright © 1977 by Austin Francis
First edition
Printed in the United States of America
123456789

U.S. Library of Congress Cataloging in Publication Data

Francis, Austin.
   Smart squash.

   1.   Squash (Game)   I.   Title.
GV1004.F7   796.34'3   77-22011
ISBN-O-397-01238-1

To my first squash teacher,
the late **Eddie Stapleton,**
a scrappy little Irishman
and squash professional
at the Princeton Club,
whose boasts, reverse corners,
and other "scintillating" shots
were once the pride
of all Boston

Contents

II
Prematch Preparation

III
Match Play

Foreword

This book has grown—I hope as a pearl from a grain of sand—out of the irritants induced when I took up the game of squash racquets.

Squash for me has been a very frustrating game and yet one so enthralling that I have surrendered to it with increasing fervor since I began. I began late, ten years out of college, and my first frustration was trying to learn a racquet sport after having grown up as a competitive swimmer.

Then I encountered a series of mental hazards: a weakness for exotic, low-percentage shots; a vulnerability to distraction; a lack of patience in developing a point; a fondness for whaling away at ground strokes. I was in sum much more of a hot hitter than a cool thinker on the court.

These problems, faced by many squash players, are all failings of the mind. My body was there but my head was someplace else. Not in the sense of abject daydreaming; more in the sense of missed mental opportunities.

It seemed to me, at one point, if I could just sort out the various disciplines which operate at the top levels of the game and make each a course of study, that I would have a curriculum for the complete squash player. And that to take each course, and take it seriously, would produce, in fact, a smart squash player.

So I have tried to do this. I have tried it in the way of a book, and I have tried it on the court. The early signs are that I am on to something, for on the day that I handed in the first draft of the manuscript, that same evening I won the David C. Johnson Memorial Handicap. I had played in this tournament for the past eight years and had never gotten beyond the round of thirty-two.

I do not aspire to be a Khan, but there are a lot of things about this game which appeal to me which I think can make me yet a better player than I am. I have enjoyed trying to define them, and I hope that, together, you and I can soon be playing very smart squash.

Austin Francis

Introduction

This excellent book should delight all squash players and others with an interest in the order of sports. Even more important, they will leave the book better players than before.

Squash can be played at many levels of intensity and, as this book so ably demonstrates, the output quality that emerges from the input is directly related to the player's personality, ability, and, above all, persistence. The great credit of Austin Francis's book is that it will benefit every player, regardless of the environmental and genetic attributes they bring to the game.

Squash has been very rewarding to me in building character, and while I firmly believe in minding my own business, I would be very pleased if squash helped to develop more fully the latent potential of others. This book is the ideal foundation for such an undertaking. It provides a distillation of the wisdom gleaned from five championship players of thoroughly disparate styles and two dedicated teachers—all keenly involved in various aspects of the game. These are all thrown into Austin Francis's still, and out comes a wonderful essence. My feeling is that the major long-term impact of this essence will be to set a handful of players on the road to greatness, as opposed to providing a middling benefit for every player.

The highest goal for me has been to create value. Business is the driving force that creates value for the masses. Nowhere do we find material well-being and personal freedom on a large scale where business is not free to seek a profit by satisfying its customers. Nowhere are these principles better illustrated than in the current developments in the world of squash.

For many years squash has been a rich man's game, with play restricted to private clubs where all women and the average man were second-class citizens. Had this situation persisted, I am convinced that squash would have been dead by 1985. But two profit-making developments rescued the game.

The first was the development of the commercial center. Sparked by their desire to make a profit, two heroic entrepreneurs—Harry Saint in New York and Paul Monaghan in Philadelphia—opened up the game to the masses. For the first time in the history of squash, women, children, and beginners are now welcome to play so long as they derive a value greater than the price our heroes must charge to satisfy them.

In conjunction with this, Colgate-Palmolive through its subsidiary, Bancroft, decided to invest more money in squash. Their investment could be profitable only if more people took up the game. This has led gradually to better facilities, more publicity, better and lower-priced equipment, improved standards of play, better refereeing, and more gallery space.

The direct result of these two forces is that squash is now experiencing a vitality that is enlivening for all who participate. Commercial clubs are springing up in the major metropolitan areas and more and more players are increasing their satisfaction by taking up the game.

This grand book is one major by-product of the joint search for profit by the producer and for satisfaction by the squash-playing customer. I am certain that many squash players will create value for themselves by purchasing this book. And I can only hope, in this enlivening process, that the author and publisher will not be forgotten by the gods of profit, either.

Victor Niederhoffer

Seven
Smart Squash
Players

I could not have written this book on my own. Although I have the credentials on the agony side, I needed the credence on the ecstasy side. And for this, I have been fortunate in lining up the help of five champions and two teachers of champions. They have given me, collectively, the key to winning squash. And in the process, they have shown me that the qualities which go along with a winning game can go a long way toward success in other undertakings.

I would like you to meet them, my seven smart squash players, and hear from each how he or she got started in the game.

Peter Briggs

Securities Broker, Squash Professional
National Intercollegiate Champion 1974–75
National Singles Champion 1976
Mexican National Singles Champion 1976
U.S. and Canadian Doubles Champion 1976,
  with Ralph Howe

"I began racquet sports with tennis at age six. Ten years later I took up squash at Middlesex Academy. I played one year of tennis at Harvard, and then about halfway through my sophomore year I decided to take squash seriously. I was right on the split between tennis and squash, but I decided that in a way I'd sort of blown it with tennis, because if I really wanted to play good top tennis, I wouldn't have gone to an Eastern college. So I quit playing tennis and just started concentrating on squash.

"So I played my junior year, and won the intercollegiates my junior year, and again my senior year. I was captain of the Harvard team my senior year, and I've kept up playing the tournaments since then. I won the National Singles Championships in 1976 and the Mexican Championships, then the U.S. and Canadian Doubles with Ralph Howe and then turned professional.

"I would like to see the game open up and grow. If the best amateurs turn pro, it will put a lot of pressure on the **15** tournaments to become open tournaments. They will have to go out and get sponsors, money, and publicity and then invite the players. With the substantial growth in numbers of courts and people taking up the game, commercial sponsors are coming into the game. This is just the way it happened with tennis."

Betty Constable

Women's Squash Coach, Princeton University
National Women's Singles Champion 1950, 1956–59

Betty's mother, Margaret Howe, was the first women's national squash champion in 1929. Young Betty was introduced to squash when she was ten, but only on a bribe basis—a pack of chewing gum to go play with her sister. She was not serious about squash until she was twenty-two and noticed that her cousin had gotten to the quarterfinals in the nationals.

"In my first nationals in 1949 I got to the finals with a very strong, bull-in-the-china-shop game, and then I won in 1950. The following year I lost in the finals, and then had three kids in three years. I loved the game so much that I went back when my children were three, two, and one. John Conroy, the Princeton coach, arranged it. I was on the roster as B. Constable. He'd sneak me in through the back door of Dillon gym. I had the last court. He told his players not to give me an inch because I was practicing for the nationals. It whipped me into excellent shape. I had to play the perfect shot because the courts were hot and the boys were fast. The corner shot had to be the perfect corner shot. Otherwise, they would come in and kill it. It must have worked because I won four straight years, 1956 to '59."

17

Betty became the first women's squash coach at Princeton in 1972, and her teams have made a 53 to 3 record since then, with four national titles in a row.

Goldie Edwards

Associate Professor of Health and Physical Education,
  The University of Pittsburgh
Canadian Women's Open Champion 1970–71
National Senior Champion 1975–77
Three-time national finalist, nationally ranked
  since 1967, currently No. 3

"I started playing squash mainly out of frustration because there was no competitive badminton in Pittsburgh. I was playing in badminton tournaments in other parts of the country and wasn't getting any practice at home. When I first went on the squash courts, I couldn't believe how dangerous it was. I thought I was going to lose my head. I stalled and sulked around for another year, then decided I had better try it again.

"I went over to the courts and this time I stuck with it. Those were very hard times. I remember the person I was playing somehow kept hitting the ball into the corner, and I thought, 'How un*fair!*' I had never played a game where the ball came off the walls, but at least I'd been part of the New Zealand junior tennis development program and had played tennis and badminton for many years, so I had that advantage.

"Gradually I found that I was getting a feedback that I was enjoying. I found that I could think about the shots and then go in and just practice them. It was sort of **19** coming around. I became a student of the game because I get a tremendous satisfaction from doing things right. So now when I'm playing good squash, it's a complete fulfillment. I think, 'Oh, how marvelous this is, it's fantastic!' I just sort of sparkle."

Cal MacCracken

President, Calmac Manufacturing Corporation
National Doubles Champion 1951, with Diehl Mateer
New York State Champion 1948–49, 1952, 1954–55, 1957–58
Metropolitan Champion 1951–54, 1959
National Veteran's Champion 1960–63
National Senior Champion 1970–72

"I grew up in a tennis family. I started playing at five because I wanted to beat my ten-year-old sister. It took me four years to do that. Dad was president of Vassar at the time, and I remember the squash courts he put in the new gym, but I never played on them. That was the first time, by the way, that girls ever had their own squash courts.

"It wasn't until I was playing tennis for Princeton that I accepted a teammate's invitation to play squash. I tried it and loved it. At first I couldn't keep myself straight. I got dizzy on the court, looking around at all the white walls and black marks. But I soon sorted it out and got fascinated by it.

"From then on I was a two-racquet man, and have played both games ever since. I find them a good switch for the seasons. Unlike some players, I think tennis and squash help each other. I don't have any trouble going from one to the other, the racquets are so different—thanks mainly to the handles. If you put a big **21** handle on a squash racquet, then I think it would be very confusing. The smaller handle is my tactile signal to make a wrist shot instead of an arm stroke.

"Also, it's hard to run around your backhand in squash."

Vic Niederhoffer

Investment Banker, Squash Professional
National Junior Champion 1962
National Intercollegiate Champion, 1964
National Singles Champion 1966, 1972–75
North American Open Champion 1975
National Doubles Champion 1968, 1973–74
  with Victor Elmaleh, James Zug, and Colin Adair

"My racquets beginnings go back to when I was six months old, crawling around an emptied-out pool in Brighton Beach Baths in Brooklyn, New York. The pool was emptied during the winter, and my parents played paddle tennis and hand tennis in this pool, which I believe is the largest in the world. They would put me down at one end of it and I would crawl all the way to the other end to try to get to their court. At the moment that I got to the court, they would pick me up and take me back to where I started from. Since that time I've entered many courts, but I've never found one as difficult to enter as that one.

"I played steadily at paddleball and handball until I was about ten and then took up tennis. At Harvard in 1961 I was introduced to the game of squash by the great coach Jack Barnaby. In the next year I had won the national junior championships and two years later had emerged as the second or third best player in men's competition in the country. In 1966 I won the amateur tour- **23** nament. In 1967 at the University of Chicago I found that I could not play in any of the local clubs there because they didn't wish to have me as a member. I believe they found me different in several aspects from their other players.

I communicated my feelings to the American Association (the championships were to be held in Chicago that year), that I didn't want to play in a tournament where I couldn't be treated as an equal. They met this situation with supreme indifference. So I went into a sort of retirement that year, and came back four years later and played in the nationals in Detroit. I won that without the loss of a game, which was the beginning of four straight years as national champion.

"I enjoy seeing young people take up squash. It's a great game to mold good qualities of mind and body. I'm certainly starting my family early. My daughter is seventeen months old and she's already been "playing" the game for over a year. She crawls from one wall to the other, chases the ball around, and can already hold a little racquet in her hand."

Norm Peck

Assistant Coach, Men's Squash and Tennis,
  Princeton University
Princeton's nine-man team, coached by Dave Benjamin
  with Peck assisting, is currently national
  intercollegiate champion. Its No. 1 player,
  Tom Page, is National Singles Champion.

"When I was a student at Trenton State about six years ago, I had been playing a lot of basketball and was looking for something different. A friend and I noticed the squash courts at the Trenton YMCA, where I worked part time, and thought it looked like a lot of fun, so we borrowed a couple of racquets and tried it.

"From the moment I got on the court I enjoyed it. Even though we had no concept of strategy, no idea where the ball was to go, we both had no trouble hitting the ball. It was just a hit-and-run operation. And yet it got to the point that, if possible, I would have played squash eight hours a day. I mean, that's how excited I got about the game.

"In gradual steps I played better players, learned basic shots, started teaching a junior program, and began studying the game seriously myself with Bill Summers, who was at that time Princeton squash coach and the only player in the Trenton area who was any kind of shot-maker. This led to an offer of a part-time assistant **25** coaching job at Princeton, and even though I had to give up my full-time job as physical director at the Y, I took it.

"Within the past few years, working for Coach Dave Benjamin, former Harvard racquet star, and being part of the Princeton squash program, I've found my game and teaching improving steadily, so that I now feel very confident in playing with and coaching any player we have here at the University."

Rick Rescigno

Squash Professional,
  Princeton Club of New York
Rescigno has established himself as a winning coach of
  executives taking up the game. His "D" teams have
  won more league championships than those of any other
  New York City professional.

"I started in this game about fifteen years ago under Lou Ballato, the City Athletic Club squash pro. My high school buddy Bob Martinez had to do six months in the Navy Reserves and wanted someone he trusted to hold his job as Lou's assistant until he got back.

"When Bob asked me if I would be interested in the job, my first reaction was, 'What's a squash pro?' I was working for a produce company at the time and I thought it must be some kind of job in the club's kitchen. Bob said not to worry, that I should come on down and he'd show me. Well, I go down, Bob introduces me, and Lou says, 'Go in with Bob and hit a couple of balls, and let's see what you can do.' So, we go onto the court, and I say to Bob, 'Gee, I don't know how this is going to work, it looks like a tough game.' I had played a little tennis and basketball but nothing like this.

"So Bob says, 'Come on, Lou's in the office. You just stand over there in the corner and watch.' Now Bob was a very good player and he got the ball going, hitting it up **27** and down the rail by himself, and he kept saying, 'That's it, Rick! Good shot! Get under that one there, that's it!' And Lou heard the ball banging around in there and he figured, 'The kid must be pretty good.' Bob and I come up and he says, 'I think everything will work out fine. He'll pick up the game. He's a good athlete.' So Lou agreed, and that's how I stopped selling and started teaching squash.''

I
Perspectives on the Game

There Goes
a Squash Player

What sort of people do you meet playing squash? You see them more these days, with their long, flat cases or their skinny racquet handles sticking out of gear bags. What are they like? The ones really hooked on the game?

Professionally, there seem to be a lot of individualists. People whose jobs are demanding, more because of the demands they place on themselves than for any other reason. Whether they be bankers, editors, small business owners, or whatever, a disproportionately high number of avid squash players seem self-driven both on and off the court.

Intellectually, players who have stronger quantitative than verbal skills seem to do better, in the sense that they tend to be more systematic and analytical with the game. **31**

Emotionally, there appears to be no common characteristic among squash players. Some, as Vic Niederhoffer observes, "get themselves into fever pitch when they play, so they can't consider anything else besides the importance and singular nature of winning. They're tense. They're unilaterally concerned with particular victory. Other players are very patient, methodical, and willing to wait for opportunities. They have a certain nonchalance on the court. Those would seem to be the two major extremes of personalities that play the game. As to where I put myself, I am very close to the opposite of fever pitch. I never get angry on the court. I'm generally very patient, self-contained, not too emotive relative to other players, concerned mainly with cultivating my own garden and playing as well as I can."

Vic also comments on some of the qualities he has observed generally in squash players: "The main qualities that are required to become a good squash player are similar to those which determine success in other fields: health, persistence, businesslike habits of organization, and a modicum of mental and physical ability. Because of this, if you have what it takes to be a good squash player, you probably have what it takes to be successful in the other things you try."

For many players, squash becomes an integral part of their routines. Bill Robinson, for example, has averaged about 250 times a year in the court for over forty years, and has described his feelings of dedication to the game in an article which appeared in the *New York Times*: "That half hour of intense concentration on the little black ball zinging around four white walls like a drunken bumblebee is the greatest antidote there is for whatever bugs you about the rest of the world. Squash releases tensions and aggressions, works out poisons, gives the most concentrated workout you can get for the time spent, keeps you out of three-martini lunches, supposedly improves your sex life—and is also just plain fun. It literally has 'all the angles,' and fanatics like me feel that its complex fascinations are unmatched in the racquet world."

The pressure on court to make instant choices among shot alternatives helps develop off-court mental acuity and indeed can encourage a certain spontaneity of character. There is a story about Germain Glidden when he was a student at Harvard. He had just won his third straight national championship and was returning on the train to New York City. He got off at Grand Central Station and was heading for the Harvard Club when he passed a theatrical costume store and an idea grabbed him. He went in, bought a moustache, goatee, graying, and glasses, made himself up, and went to the Yale Club, where he introduced himself to the squash pro, Ed Standing, as a beginner and asked for a lesson.

Standing and Glidden went on the court, and Glidden, a lefty, played with his right hand. Every once in a while, when Standing was up front, Glidden would switch hands and bang the ball by him. The pro couldn't believe it. After the lesson Glidden asked for a game, and when three or four points had been played, he switched permanently to his left hand, gradually picking up the pace until he had Standing lying in a heap in the corner, and he was lying in another corner doubled up in laughter, with the pieces of his disguise scattered nearby. All Standing could say was, "Why, Mr. Glidden!"

Germain Glidden enjoyed himself tremendously that way. He was very alert, superquick. His reaction times were so fast that he stood 3 or 4 feet further up than most players. He loved the straight drops, the front-wall nicks, and the crazy angles. He was so quick he could do all these things. If you saw him going down the street, his body angled forward and his eyes taking in everything that came in range, you could almost divine: "There goes a squash player . . ."

Learning from a Professional

The majority of the estimated 500,000 North American squash players today play in private or public clubs, and in most of those clubs there is a squash professional. These professionals can be credited with having taught the game to most of its regulars, many of whom had never seen a squash court until after they were out of school. I fit that description myself.

If you want to take up the game or improve your current skills, what should you expect from a squash professional? What sort of things can you learn? What do they teach you at the different levels of the game?

I asked Rick Rescigno to answer these questions, and generally to describe his approach to teaching squash. **35**

Rick, currently the squash professional at the Princeton Club of New York, has been a pro for fifteen years, and, as he puts it, "I have had them all—short and tall, skinny and fat, young and old, serious and casual, all sexes—come onto the court at one time or another wanting to learn something about the game.

"If you want to take lessons from me," says Rick, "the first thing I do is peg your game, unless I know beforehand that you are a beginner. We warm up the ball and play a few points so I can see what needs the most work. During the rally, I check your grip, strokes, and eye patterns; the angle of your shoulders, shooting elbow, and feet; and where you position the racquet head. I also try to find out what you expect from your lessons to avoid teaching you only what I think you should learn.

"If you are a beginner, I like to start by helping you develop a correct grip and a natural, rhythmic swing. First, without the ball, and usually in front of a large mirror, we both go through the motions. I try to get you to relax and feel the weight of the racquet head pulling you through the stroke into the follow-through position.

"When the stroke is executed properly, you will feel the racquet doing most of the work as if it were leading your hands through the motion. I try to get all my students to let the racquet power the ball rather than trying to muscle the ball. Squash is a game of accuracy as well as speed. Accuracy comes from touch, and touch is the result of a smooth-flowing swing.

"After I think you understand the concept of the swing, we go on the court and work on two stroking exercises which you can use later when practicing alone. The first is designed to help you 'groove' the forehand and backhand stroking motion while executing the game's basic shot, the rail. The second uses a close-in, constant hitting routine to train you to get the racquet back quickly with the head in the right position. It also develops strength in the fingers and quickness of wrist.

"If you are further along, say near or at the D level in the New York area, I usually concentrate on elementary strategy. We work on getting you to hit a reasonably safe offensive shot, keeping it well above the tin but still forcing your opponent into a difficult position. We also work on teaching you the ability to dig yourself out of such positions. So you begin to learn the two sides of the game.

"I have found too often that a D player will get the idea from watching a top-level match that the way to play the game is to do a lot of trick shooting. What they don't see is the depth process which puts the opponent in one of the corners, forces a weak return, and opens up three fourths of the court for a relatively easy winner. So what I zero in on is getting my D player to be aware that the drop shot, or any other difficult putaway, is not the shot on which the point is going to be won. That is not the ultimate shot to learn. The shot that does the job eighty percent of the time is the one which *gradually* moves an opponent into more and more trouble, and that shot is usually the rail or cross-court drive. These are your money shots in squash.

"At the C and B levels, I work on patience and persistence. On each shot, no matter how good you think it was, I try to get you to pursue the point until the ball has bounced twice, for or against you. So that where I expect a typical point in a good D match to last for about five exchanges and perhaps end with a rail followed by a drop or reverse corner, as a B player you must expect your opponent to retrieve those shots. Only by staying in the point can you pick up your opponent's 'get' and *perhaps* win the point on a cross-court drive to the farthest corner.

"My teaching method at this level is best described as a

stretching program, which is actually true to a degree in any of my lessons. That is, I keep the ball always a foot or so beyond where you can reach it comfortably. And I make you visit and revisit every part of the court. This is particularly important at the C and B levels, where the development of a point and the successful application of a strategy can frequently go beyond ten exchanges per player.

"Also, when I am with students who are seriously trying to improve their games, I generally teach by playing points only, rather than whole games. We may play a single game at the end of the lesson, but I want the student to concentrate mainly on the ideas we are working on and not get distracted by thinking, 'Oh, boy, if I make this point I've beaten Rescigno!'

"As I move on up to the A level, I try to do two things when I'm giving a lesson, or perhaps I should say 'playing with a customer,' because an A player doesn't really take lessons. At least you won't find many who will admit to it.

"If you are an A player, I bring my shots as close to the wall as possible, forcing you to do the same. I also speed up the game to make you think and act faster. I use a lot of volleys to keep you behind me if possible. This shortens the time period you have to get set on your shots and forces you to play under pressure.

"One thing I have seen many A players do when they have plenty of time to set up on the ball—they add something to their backswing, perhaps out of boredom, perhaps out of a desire to hit a real smoker. This exaggerated backswing forces errors. It may not be an obvious error like a tin; it may only be a rail shot which comes out six inches from the side wall, but at the A level this can be the opening an opponent has been waiting for. The good players, even, make this mistake a lot.

"I'd like to comment on a few players I've worked with over the past few years because I think it might give you some idea of what a squash professional tries to accomplish with different individuals.

"With women players generally, I have tried to help them overcome the frustration of not being able to hit the ball hard. If they are playing with a man or with anyone who hits very hard, I try to teach them how to convert the speed of their opponent's shot into their own shot. The ball loses only a small amount of speed if a hard shot is returned properly. A woman player using this approach will get better length and can often force errors and turn the tide against a stronger player.

"One thing I've noticed over the years in tennis and squash is that flat-chested women seem to run better. They are usually better squash players than more fully endowed women. There have been exceptions to this, but apparently women with smaller bosoms have less weight to counteract when starting and stopping. They usually can change direction a lot easier, which is an important aspect of squash.

"Also, women seem to turn at the waist a lot better than men. They are more flexible in the hips, so that they can get around on the ball with less difficulty. Because of this, most women can work themselves out of the back corners in the early stages of their learning a lot better than men. Men try to muscle the ball out of the corners. A woman will turn and instinctively try to flip the ball out of a corner, so she picks that shot up a lot quicker than a man.

"Of all the players I have taught from scratch, I think Mel Boren has been the most successful. Mel was always fairly athletic. He played baseball and a little football as a kid. After college he became a terrific golfer. So he had developed good moves and reasonably good reflexes when—in his early thirties—he first entered a squash court.

"I could tell, the way he walked on the court and the way he moved to the ball, that if he was taught properly, Mel could excel at squash. What he needed was the hand work. We had to get his racquet head set in the right position. My theory has always been that when the racquet head starts out right it will go through the ball correctly. I have found that problems in the backswing—the wrist out of position, the head too high or low, the forearm and elbow not set correctly—will rob the swing of the fluidness it needs to power the ball.

"I worked with Mel over a period of two to three years, and combined with the time he spent practicing, he rose quickly in the Metropolitan leagues to become a high-B, low-A player. Mel really wanted to learn the game. If he had not had a back problem, I think he would have been a solid A player.

"Now take Marty Cohen. He was taller and more awkward than Mel. His feet didn't work well, which affected his racquet work. Marty never got himself in good enough position to let his hands do what they were capable of doing. We worked on getting his forward foot in position, and with time, Marty made it past the average level onto a club team. This year he had a very good year in D and will probably be moved up to C.

"The type of game Marty has developed is a steady one. He's not what you'd call a great shotmaker. But because he has dealt with his target areas and worked on his feet more, he makes a hell of a lot less errors, I'd say ninety percent less. So he's a player that you have to beat. He's not going to give you too many points.

"Bill Robinson had a completely different problem, and

a very unusual one. He relearned the game with his left hand after he had been playing it right-handed for over forty years. Bill had torn a rotator cuff muscle in his right shoulder making an overhead smash following a tough tournament weekend. When his doctor told him he was going to be out a long time, if not permanently, he decided left-handed was better than having to give up his daily game, so he came to me and we started over from scratch.

"Bill had the court sense and knew what he was supposed to do, but we had to translate that knowledge into a new feeling. His sense of where his body was relative to hitting the ball from the left side was backward. He crowded the ball on his forehand and often couldn't reach it on his backhand, which made balls along the wall especially difficult for him to hit; and I remember the frustration and broken racquets he went through before this ability came to him.

"I think Bill could have become a very good left-handed player, because he had better form on the left than on the right, where he had more or less picked up the game on his own as he was growing up. He had gotten up to about the D level with his left hand when his right shoulder healed enough to let him switch back, so we'll never find out just how good his left hand really is.

"In the days before his 'lefty' expertise left him, Bill was playing C squash with his right hand and had entered the Princeton Club handicap tournament with his left hand, which was the only way he could legally do so, having won that tournament right-handed a few years earlier. He was even threatening to apply for a simultaneous left-D, right-C ranking in the Metropolitan Squash Racquets Association."

Developing Your Own Style

There must be as many distinguishable styles in squash as there are personalities of players. In effect, a person's style of play becomes an extension of his or her physical and emotional makeup.

As your game progresses, you will want to select certain things to work on which will enable you to develop the strongest personal style.

One way of selecting aspects of the game you wish to incorporate into your own game is by watching good squash. Goldie Edwards tells how she does this: "When I go to a big tournament like the North American Open, I'm never just a pure spectator. I go to learn how to play better. I can model, I can copy. So, if somebody does something, I will say, 'Oh, yeah, I had forgotten about that. That will really help me in my next match.'

"I follow the player, not the ball, with my eyes. I'm watching him to see how he's hitting, to see how quickly he gets his racquet back, how far he takes it back, what he does with it, how he comes through, how he gets power, how his feet and shoulders are. I watch all those things to see if there's something I'm not doing. I look for individual techniques and stroke production.

"When I'm watching for strategy, then I have to look at it globally, that is, the court at large. I see both players now. I see the pattern, I see what shot was followed with what. I make a quick decision if it was good or not.

"Watching these top players, I can see how much *hustle* is required sometimes to get to the ball. If I'm in close, I can see the *determination* which supports this hustle. You really have to get there *fast* and make a *thing* of it. And it's good to be reminded of that every so often."

At the beginning of his professional career, Rick Rescigno picked up the various parts of his repertory by watching different New York City club pros as they gave lessons. "I used to go to all the clubs, because I had to carry the squash bags if there was a team match. This gave me the chance to see guys like Frank Iannicelli, who at the time was a big name in the game, and Ray Widelski, who was then on his way up. I used to watch Johnny Greco, Tommy Burns. Each guy had his own particular style—the way he moved to the ball, how he hit it—and it helped me develop my own style. I took a little bit from everybody and experimented to see exactly which style would be best for me, and what I could adapt easily into a strong, consistent game.

"For a long time I used to stroke like Mohibullah Khan. I used his very short grip and full backswing to get the length that forced my opponents back and let me get up front. With the shortened-up grip, my racquet was a surgeon's scalpel. I could flick the ball this way and that. Those were the Cragin Green Diamond days, when we used a ball that suited the style I had developed.

"Then the ball changed, and so did my Mo Khan style. The West Company Blue Dot was a much faster, bouncier ball. I had to lengthen my grip and move back in the court and concentrate more on consistently deep shots. It was a less interesting style, but if I could keep the ball in the back corners and was patient, then I could still get up front for all the exotic shots I love to hit."

Betty Constable is another player who changed styles during her career. When she first began competing at the national level, she had a power game. "Babe Bowles beat me in the finals of my first nationals. I was big and I really hit the ball then. I had been told that I had the upper hand if I was on the T. They told me, 'You get on that T, come hell or high water, you get on that T.' Well, I did, and Babe gave it to me. But then she dumped everything from the back wall—drops, corners, you name it. There I was on the T, ready to go, and all these shots were coming out of nowhere. That was 1949.

"By the time I came back from semiretirement and began playing again, I had had the advantage of a two-month tour to Europe on the Women's Wolfe-Noel Team. And then the British women players came to this country. They had been told they could destroy us by hitting hard. I found out when playing them here that the only way I could beat them was to make shots even when I didn't want to, because they didn't expect them. So this became my new style. I practiced my shots a lot then, and it was the way I held onto the national title for four straight years.

"I remember a match against Margaret Varner in my last year of tournament play. She was the up-and-coming queen and was beating everybody. She was very aggressive on the court. I had heard from somebody that she said she was going to beat me. As soon as we began, she took charge of the T. And I said, 'Okay, now I'm going to show her.' I think I pulled every shot I knew against her, my back-wall shots, drops, corners, all kinds of dump shots. Margaret was furious. I taught her the same lesson Babe Bowles had taught me.''

A clash of contrasting styles, even when the differences are subtle, is a common ingredient in squash matches. Knowing your own style, what your strengths are, and being able to play consistently up to your potential against other styles of play is one of the most difficult challenges of the game.

Style is a topic that turns Peter Briggs on. Ask him what shots his opponent is going to use and you'll get, "Everybody in the game has the same shots." Ask what strategies he is going to use: "I'm just going to play." But ask him what he thinks of a particular opponent's style, and you're likely to get a monologue of some depth and passion: "Niederhoffer and I are totally at opposite ends of the spectrum. I think his style is perfect for him. And I think my style is perfect for me. He is obviously successful, as his record shows. On the other hand, I feel confident of my ability to equal that record, and just do it another way.

"Vic is very clinical and I'm very emotional. I play either very well or very badly. I don't have any middle ground. And he pretty much always sort of glides along at a particular level, at a very fine level. He is more methodical than I am, and he has better concentration than I do. So therefore my game goes in ups and downs.

"On the other hand, I think Vic's kind of game has a limit. It has a cap on it just in the way that it is conceived.

Because it *is* so analytical. It is not subject to great lows, and it is not subject to great highs.

"When I am emotionally right and playing at my best, I don't think there is anyone who can touch me. On those days I can play a little faster and handle my racquet a little better than my opponents. The challenge for me now, as I approach my peak playing years, is to gain the concentration to do that more often.

"My approach to the game will probably hurt me as I get older, where a guy like Niederhoffer, with his style, can play at the top level well into his thirties. Sooner or later I've got to slow down. But I couldn't switch styles, because then I would be changing my personality."

Winning Strategies for Veteran Players

It should comfort older squash players to note that, in the 1977 Boodles Gin Squash Challenge Series, the median age of the ten professionals competing for the prize is thirty-two. And that among them are Sharif Khan, who at thirty-two is the premier player in North America, followed by Vic Niederhoffer and Rainer Ratinac at thirty-three, Frank Satterthwaite at thirty-four, Khalid Mir at thirty-five, and Mohibullah Khan at thirty-seven.

If so many top-ranked players are well into their thirties, there must be something about squash, other than strength and endurance, which defines excellence. I think there is, and I believe that this special ingredient is a combination of complexity and finesse which takes longer to master than in most other sports. Take one small example: in tennis there is no such thing as a nick **47** or a ball so tight to the wall that it is simply unhittable. But in squash both exist, they are outright winners, and they may be mastered by players who stick with the game. And significantly, neither shot depends on power.

The conclusion I have drawn from these observations is: an older player who is willing to master shot selection and shot execution can often win over a more agile, harder-hitting opponent. The older player must be in reasonably good condition, of course, but even if there is a modest endurance gap in favor of the younger player, it can often enough be overcome by an intelligent, consistent game.

Vic Niederhoffer agrees: "One of the distinguishing features of squash is that a mid-level player with good skills can overcome a physical disadvantage in terms of strength or agility. I would say that an average player with good finesse, anticipation, diversification, and concentration should beat an opponent who is ten to twenty percentage points higher on various physical tests."

I asked Norm Peck to imagine that he is talking to a team of graduate players in their thirties or older who are getting ready to play the Princeton undergraduates, and to lay out what he feels will be a winning strategy. Here it is: "I want you to practice two things this week on the return of serve. Either you will hit a reverse corner or, if you're not comfortable with that, I want you to neutralize the serve by bringing it carefully down the line with good length to force your man into a defensive situation. No cross-courts off the serve, until you catch him leaning into your rail shot, and nothing hard.

"Secondly, I want you to concentrate on shotmaking: your serve, a defensive lob, and finishing shots such as a three-wall nick, straight or cross-court drop, or a roll corner.

"The outcome of most of your matches is going to depend on your shotmaking ability and your being able to dictate the flow of the match. You can do this if you realize that some of these kids have played squash for only a couple of years. Although they are good athletes, your experience will help you to use the entire court to your advantage. The main strategy is to leave your shots in one of the four corners of the court, keeping the ball from coming back out toward the center. Make your opponents cover a tremendous amount of court, completely twisting and changing direction within the course of a point. You do this and, unless your man is awfully quick and has excellent shotmaking skills of his own, you're going to be dictating the points and the match."

From the point of view of one who has been there, here is Cal MacCracken telling you some of the secrets that have contributed to one of the all-time great veteran squash records: "The older squash players can use intelligence and their knowledge of the game to better effect than in a lot of other sports. There's always something new to learn in squash. That's one of the things that intrigues me about it. You can learn a stroke refinement every year.

"When you get to be my age and your reflexes aren't quite as fast, you can't turn quite as far—your knees aren't that strong—you can't reach quite as far, and so on, you *have* to make a refinement. The main thing I have done is learn to lob well, because in getting to the ball I am often a step behind, and it is important to get out front and get your opponent behind you.

"You're usually not in a position to hit hard cross-court returns at the younger players. So I have learned to keep a lob along the wall so close that my opponent has to let them drop down and take them in the rear corner. Then I can move up to the front of the court. This is the main thing I rely on now when I play younger players.

"Also I try to rattle a younger player with variety. For example, hard serves that come out into the middle. Hard serves aiming for the corner nick. I give them balls at different angles, speeds, with different English, trajectories, and heights. I also volley every time I can to stay out front. I try to keep them guessing as much as possible so that they don't get grooved on doing any one thing.

"When I was in my mid-thirties, I used to be known as a well-conditioned player. For example, if I were to play the intercollegiate champion, like Steve Vehslage, or some other guy like that, I would just know inside my head that I could out-condition the guy, that I could get him tired.

"The players who are of college age really are not yet, most of them, in condition for real tough squash. It's just like the marathon runners. They are never college kids. You have to develop the lung capacity and everything that goes with it, and you rarely do this by age twenty. It's usually by age twenty-five, or more, that you develop these things, and they will last quite well, I think, up into the mid-thirties. So that I beat most of those young kids who had fantastic strokes, much better than mine, by tiring them out. I knew I couldn't win in three games, that it would be four or five.

"I remember playing Bob Hetherington, then a top Yale player. He used to come down and lose to me, and it really killed him. He once said to me, 'I can't believe it, Cal, you're older than my father!'"

When a Woman Plays a Man

Even when you filter out or ignore the roses-on-the-court and other Riggsian extranea, there is still a residual nonsquash difference that hovers over the court when a woman plays a man.

Vic Niederhoffer, when advising a woman on male-opponent strategy, says, "Get in good condition. Try to develop short shots as fast as you can, early in your learning rather than at the end." But then he adds, "Beg for mercy."

It's hard to get away from *la différence*. But as the popularity of squash grows, there are more and more serious female/male encounters, especially at the lower metropolitan-league levels. So what can you do as a woman if you want to beat a man?

Betty Constable has a number of tricks in her bag **51**

which she has used against male opponents. I have been the victim of a few of them myself. One of her pet peeves is the surrender by women of privileged court space: "A lot of girls today don't take enough room on the court, especially against a male opponent. Donald Strachan taught me how to back a man against the wall and then step back into the shot. I leave my rear foot out, too. That holds him back another two feet. Sometimes he gets so mad it's worth a couple of extra points."

Betty is also a big advocate of hitting a shot which for most players carries a higher degree of risk. This of course means that a woman typically must play with greater control than a man. "When a man was faster and stronger," she says, "I had to be brainier and more accurate. The only thing I could do was play the shot before he played it, at every opportunity, whether I wanted to or not. I avoided marathons and went for the winner before he did. I was known among women players as a shotmaker. And I figured that was the only way to beat the men. It's much easier to bang the ball up and down the wall and cross-court, because it's safer. But I've always maintained, if you're out in front, on the T, you should go for a shot. And, sometimes, when you're not on the T, when he's least expecting it, you should hit the shot.

"And changes of pace," Betty continues, "that's another thing most men don't understand. They never expect a change of pace from anybody, like a drop, or a reverse corner off the rear wall. Shots from behind a guy really devastate him. One of my favorite winners against men was a cross-court drop after an exchange of hard shots. They were *never* ready for it."

Goldie Edwards plays most of her squash in Pittsburgh, where there aren't any top-ranked women. So she gets her competition from the men. "The A players call me to play. They seem to like playing with me, maybe because I run them. I make them move. A lot of the fellows say they get a better workout with me than with many of the other people they play regularly.

"Most of the men I play really power the ball—they try to blast me off the court. Sometimes they are really big, so that I must dodge around behind them to reach the ball. I can usually get around and get my racquet in there. I make out all right.

"I find the best way to beat a man is to play more shots than he does, to give him the unexpected. I play a lot of soft stuff, but mostly off the back wall. Or, if I can catch it on the half volley, then I will dump it.

"To play well against a man, you have to develop control, and the essence of control is keeping it along the wall. Very often, if I'm scrambling and reaching, what I can do is just lift one, very softly, that's really tight to the wall. It's sort of a half lob. It takes the speed off the ball and slows up the pace. If they boast and it nicks, then I'm dead, but if it doesn't, then I can usually put it away.

"I use the lob as an offensive shot. Almost nobody lobs, except to dig themselves out of a hole. I can do it very easily because my grip is correct. I can be reaching for a ball up front, and either touch it for a drop or flick it up for a lob. Same thing on the backhand. I find it *very* effective. When it's really tight to the wall, they almost break their racquets trying to hit it.

"There was one man I played several years ago who recently came up to me at a luncheon and reminded me of the match we had played. He said, 'You know, I have never been beaten in anything by a woman, before or since.' I had forgotten both his name and face, but my victory still stuck in his craw. Why is it that some men have the nerve to think they have a natural right to win? Or, more puzzling to me, why do some women have a built-in thing that they must lose to a man?"

Sex Before Squash?

The question arises more frequently now, both with the growth of participant sports and with the entry of women into formerly male-dominated sports: Does sex before play improve your game? There are some strongly held views on the subject, and there have been at least a couple of recent magazine articles by physicians which reflect a net positive view toward the effects of sex on athletic performance.

Reliable research is hard to come by on this subject. Had Masters and Johnson been squash players, we might not still be up in the air over the solution to this intriguing problem.

However, until such time as a definitive study is made, I have run across an excellent sample of one, a former world class squash player who has run tests on himself and has come to the conclusion that he should abstain from sex for forty-eight hours before a serious match. I asked him to explain how he had arrived at this conclusion.

"Some people say that sex helps your game, but I think that's a lot of baloney. Unless it is an individual difference, which I doubt. I think if a person were to test it scientifically as I have done, he or she would find that the amount of physical effort you can expend after sex is significantly less than before. I have come to this conclusion by taking certain physical tests such as push-ups and sprints, before and after. In addition, before several of the matches that I have lost, prior to my tests, I had violated this principle.

"Naturally, you tend to hear about the exceptional cases, where someone who has just set a new record or played particularly well has had sex beforehand. They are certainly more prone to talk about it than if they had lost. There is a generally held desire to believe that sex and winning are complementary. It titillates people to think so. It's in line with male aspirations and a macho point of view—the 'I don't give a damn' outlook.

"While it is correct to have a certain evenness of temper, so that you can be within your own values while you're playing, you also have to have a certain tension and desire to achieve, a momentum and persistence. I don't think there's any question that after someone has had sex, he or she is pretty tired and relaxed, which is antithetical to one of the major states necessary for victory. For example, try to get into a fever pitch after dallying, unless you dally without consummation, and that's something I haven't explored."

I asked this squash player if he were exploring the matter further and he said, "At my age, one leaves that sort of scientific experimentation to readers of your book and others of an inquisitive nature."

For Americans Who Play English

Only a few years ago the English ball was unknown to most American players. A few expatriate Londoners might have brought a ball over in their duffle hoping to find a kindred spirit. But such were rare.

As an historical aside, the American game was imported from England in the late 1800s and then made formal in 1907, with standard court dimensions, a national association, and the first national championships. The English game, though older, was not standardized until the late 1920s. There have been sporadic but unsuccessful attempts to bring the two together. The facilities, the balls, and the inherent characteristics of the two games are too different to permit a merger without one or both sides submitting to an unacceptable degree of trauma.

However, as the game of squash racquets has grown in this country, more people have become year-round players. And, in the summer, the English ball has provided an ideal change of pace, both psychologically and physically, which has helped keep players alert and interested—at least in New York and several other major squash centers.

In the meantime, for those who switch from ball to ball, I asked Peter Briggs, who lately has played more English squash than any other top-ranked American, to give his views on the major differences confronting Americans who intermittently play the English game.

"The American and English games are very different psychologically. For Americans to adapt well to the English ball, they must understand these differences, and I think a good way to understand them is to view them as typical of the American and English mentalities.

"The English game is a game of attrition. It is the slow erosion of another player. To play it well, you have to subtly and patiently break down your opponent. To enjoy watching the English game you have to appreciate this characteristic also. Actually, though I enjoy playing the English game, I think it is a totally boring game to watch. People don't enjoy watching one guy gradually work another into the ground. A top-level, five-game match in English squash is grueling. You can have exchanges of twenty, thirty, and even forty shots for every point, and the match can last for two and a half hours.

"On the other hand, with the American game, a five-game match is usually over in an hour and fifteen minutes. That's a good span of attention for spectators, and it's one reason why commercial sponsors are getting into the American game. It's very promotable as a spectator sport.

"The American mentality loves the element of violence

in contact, the intensity, the quick action, the big play—all of these are more pronounced in American squash than they are in English. We owe these to our smaller court and faster ball.

"Looking at the two games as a strategist, in the English you get two guys out there and they beat their heads together for two hours, and suddenly one guy's just not there any more. You won't see that in American squash. You'll see two guys beating their heads together, and one guy will lose, but he'll be able to walk out. Because it's a shot-oriented game. In American squash it is physically possible to hit forty-five three-wall nicks in a row. It could happen, and you'd have your guy out of there in fifteen minutes.

"That's not going to happen in the English game. There are fewer kill shots and you don't get any cheap points. Even if your opponent mis-hits, unless it is totally erratic, you can still get it. So a guy who is in real good condition but doesn't have many shots can still hang in there in the English game. But a guy in good condition without shots could get killed by an American shotmaker who is also in good condition. Because the ball can be put away.

"The next difference you should be aware of is in the strokes. The English stroke is a higher, longer stroke, because the ball is softer. So to generate pace and speed, you have to put more into it.

"The shots are different too. In the American game you aim your rails and cross-courts about six inches to a foot above the tin to get the ball past the guy. The same target in English barely makes it to the service line where the guy is standing. You have to aim the ball almost as high as the service line to get the right trajectory so it will get back far enough. And if it really gets hot—when you're really smoking it—then you can go closer to the tin.

"There is no reverse corner in the English game because the ball, due to its characteristics, just comes out into the middle. It's actually a terrible shot. It's one of the pitfalls that an American player runs into when he plays overseas. He has a pattern in his mind that every now and then calls for a reverse corner, so he hits one, and suddenly he's way out of position. Similarly, when an

Figure 1. The Workingman's Boast

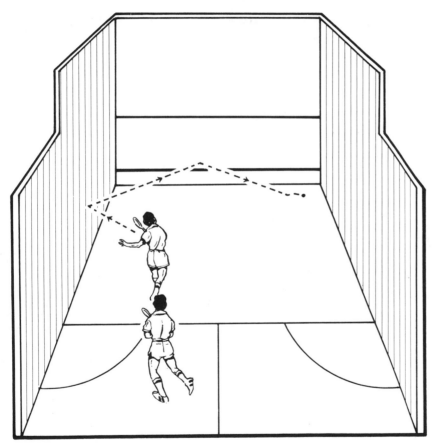

English player comes here, the reverse corner is a prime shot to hit against him because he has never seen it.

"The serve is not a weapon in English squash. The hard serve in American squash *is* a weapon. You can hit it right at the guy. You can go for the nick in the back. You can hit a criss-cross so it comes into him at an angle. But the serve in English squash is used primarily to put the ball in play.

"There's one shot in English squash where you hit the ball really hard into the side wall at right angles, and the ball goes up to the front wall and because of their wider court it just doesn't quite get to the third wall. They call this shot a 'workingman's boast' (Figure 1). All it really means is that if you hit it correctly, the guy just has to bust his butt chasing after it. The English game is centered around making the guy work, exposing whether he's in good shape or not. And with this shot, you get exposed in a hurry."

The 70+ Ball

To be in one's forties and have the official ball changed every year or two in such a shot-oriented game as squash is punishment comparable to that endured by Sisyphus. Even now, as I have gained a familiar comfort with the West Company Blue Dot, and after having been a veritable nemesis with the Cragin Green Diamond, the gods of balldom are holding council to vote on next year's pellet. Will it be the Blue Dot again, or will it be the new 70+ ball?

The gods cannot agree. As this book goes to press, the U.S. Squash Racquets Association, and its various member regions, who are the standard setters for club players, are not in full agreement over which ball to use. The professionals and intercollegians, however, have come down heavily in favor of the 70+.

Sharif Khan plays with the English ball in the summertime, but in the winter, all the major tournaments he plays in use the West Company Blue Dot. "So I have to switch back and forth, and now I'll have to switch again for the Seventy-plus," he says. When asked if the 70+ is going to be the new ball, Sharif says, "Yes, yes, there's no question about it!"

What does he think of the new ball? "With the Seventy-plus you retain quite a bit of each game. So, if you play the English game, you can still play drop shots, you can lob the ball. If you are a North American hard-ball player, and you can drill it, like I can, then you can still do that with the Seventy-plus."

Vic Niederhoffer thinks the 70+ ball will require more physical endurance at the top levels of the game. At mid-level he believes it will give players more time to think and react and for this reason will be a much better ball for women and most men players. He says, "The ball has already proved to be more satisfying to the major customers of the game than the various makes of the North American hard ball."

Norm Peck likes the 70+. "I didn't think I was going to like it as much as I do. After examining it, the first thing I thought about, immediately, was the English ball. Which I really don't like. But the fact is, every shot that you can hit with the American ball, you can hit with the Seventy-plus. The only real difference is that it doesn't hang up like the Blue Dot, so you will have to work harder to get to the ball in time.

"I think the Seventy-plus will improve shotmaking as a whole. It will definitely improve the drop shot. The lob will be more effective. You'll get more touch on the lob than you get with the Blue Dot. And the roll corner will stay down better. So that, really, the front-court game will be a much bigger factor with the Seventy-plus.

"In a match where you have two players, both in good condition, but one a better shotmaker, I think the Seventy-plus ball will widen the gap in favor of the shot-maker. It should bring an overall improvement in the level of squash skills and that, I think, will be a big boost to North American squash."

So there you have it. Here we go again. I hope no one is working on a successor to the 70+ with yet another set of playing characteristics. I sure would like to settle on a ball and perhaps develop a vintage shot or two before hanging up my sneakers.

Doubles, Anyone?

It was late one Thursday evening in March of 1961 when the phone rang in Englewood, New Jersey, at Cal Mac-Cracken's home. On the other end from Philadelphia was a deceptively calm Diehl Mateer: "Cal, how'd you like to play with me in the national doubles championships in Pittsburgh on Saturday?"

"Now Diehl, you *know* I don't play doubles!"

"That's okay, your game is sound and, besides, I'd really like you to play."

"Can't you get anyone else?"

"Well, to tell the truth," said Diehl, "my partner, Hunter Lott, is sick, and I've tried everyone else. I want to play, and I think you and I would do fine. Come on down to Merion Cricket Club tomorrow and we'll teach you how to play doubles."

64   Cal went down the next day and spent all afternoon being coached by Diehl and his father. They drove to Pittsburgh that night, and Saturday morning early they were on the court. "I remember the first point in the first match," says Cal. "Diehl was on the left and I was on the right, and without thinking I ended up over in front of him hitting a shot. 'Get over there and *stay* over there!' Diehl shouted. Now that was a command to be obeyed, and I obliged.

"Diehl is a super squash player. He hits the ball very well and hard, and he was ninety percent of our team. We had a lot of tough matches, but we went right on through to the finals, where we met Germain Glidden and Cliff Sutter.

"At one point Diehl and Germain were banging the ball up and down the left-hand wall and all of a sudden the ball came cross-court to me. I waded into it and made a beautiful reverse corner to end the point. I felt great, until I realized—aided in no small measure by the silence and Diehl's icy glare—that I had hit my own partner's cross-court shot. In the finals of the national doubles championships!"

Cal shaped up, and they went on to win the match and the title. Except for one other foray with Ed Hahn, in the national senior doubles, Cal has stayed with his stock-in-trade singles game ever since.

The beauty of doubles is that it can prolong the pleasures of playing competitive squash well into maturity.

According to Bill Robinson, who has played doubles regularly for over forty years, "The game is a leveler because you are only playing on one side, you have a longer time to react, and solid defensive shots are an important part of the game. A player with good, steady shots can make a contribution. It's not necessary to hit a lot of spectacular winners."

The main differences between squash doubles and singles are, briefly:

- The court is *more* than double the size of a singles court in terms of cubic measurement, 138 percent larger, to be exact.
- The ball is heavier and a lot livelier.
- The racquet should be slightly heavier.

Doubles is a game of positioning. Each team plays to move the other team out of position. Winners per stroke are much less frequent than in singles. There is a lot of defensive shooting and maneuvering of opponents before the opening for a winner can be developed. Hence the points are longer.

A typical winner in doubles is a passing shot at about shoulder level that doesn't come far enough off the back wall to recover. You can eventually make short shots when you get both of your opponents back behind the red line. To back them off you must play deep to the corners.

The length of a doubles court is a bigger factor in scoring points than in singles. Thus, if you run up front for a drop shot in doubles, you are farther out of position than you would be in singles.

Instead of controlling the T, your team must control the red line across its entire width. If you are both on the red line and you have a clear shot, then you're in good shape.

Singles players taking up doubles must master the rotational procedure before their accustomed expertise can be transferred completely to the new game. That is, they must learn to hit and rotate out of the way of the opponent on their side. This is not the same as clearing in singles. It is a more courtly maneuver, usually conducted in a consistently clockwise or counterclockwise direction. It is both cooperative and competitive at the same time and, between two accomplished teams, it lends a certain grace and decorum to the game of doubles which enhance its appeal.

In Squash, Two's a Crowd

When Hashim Khan first came over to this country, he used to take a *big* follow-through after a very hard-hitting shot. In the English game, because the ball moves slower and the court is larger, it isn't so important to stand close together. You can give a little more room. So Khan was used to taking a big follow-through.

Diehl Mateer was playing Khan in the semi's of the first national open championship. Cal MacCracken was there and gives this report: "Mateer was determined to win, so he was standing his ground, allowing himself to be hit repeatedly on Khan's follow-through. The racquet head was coming around and hitting Mateer on the leg. I went into the shower with him after the third game and counted twenty-three racquet welts all up and down his right leg, some still showing the impression of the strings. He eventually lost the match, and Henri Salaun beat Khan in the finals on the following day."

The effects of crowding in squash are not always so damaging, but because of the game's speed and its narrow confines, understanding and being able to cope with the physical proximity of your opponent are crucial to success.

Under most playing conditions, crowding is a state of mind that does not include physical contact or even a let call. It is rather a discomfort or stress that players feel when getting set to stroke that causes them to hit a slightly rushed or cramped shot. As Peter Briggs says, "There's a difference between playing competitively close to a guy, so you can reach his better shots, and downright hanging all over him. By playing him close, it also adds a little bit more intensity. Lots of guys personally don't like this, your breathing down their necks. It bugs them."

Diehl Mateer not only got close to his opponents when they were hitting; he also knew how to keep them away when it was his turn. Again, MacCracken is the observer: "When you go in against Mateer, he takes his room to take his shot. There's nothing wrong with that. It's perfectly legal. And you *give* it to him. He sticks his rear end *way* out and you find yourself backed flat against the wall when you don't want to be over there. And you wouldn't be over there with most other players because they wouldn't be taking any more room than they actually needed."

A common mistake caused by crowding occurs when you are backing into an area being vacated by your opponent. You have a good bead on the ball but you take your eye off it to see if the way is clear. Now you've got to re-bead before hitting and you hit the tin. "There is no reason for this," says Betty Constable. "You're *not* supposed to be thinking about your opponent. It's just between you and the ball. You have enough work to do to think about that ball and what you're going to do with it."

There are players who take unfair advantage of the court space. They push you around. After a certain amount of this, you have to push back and call let or you will lose. With players who take up too much of the court space, you've got to train yourself to call let *before* you hit the shot. That's rather hard for a lot of people to do. They can't make the decision that they are being interfered with *fast* enough. It all happens in a fraction of a second, and if you don't call let you are giving your opponent the advantage. The good players don't hit balls even when they are only *mildly* interfered with. They don't hit until their opponent starts adhering to the rules.

In league matches or other nontournament competition, where there is often no referee, there is almost no case where you wouldn't get a let when you call one. Or, you can always ask for a referee if nothing else works.

When your opponent unnecessarily or continually interferes with your shots, you should ask for a let point. Vic Niederhoffer is in favor of awarding let points even when a player has hit a bad shot and is *unable* to clear. "It will *improve* the game, because most of the time I have found a very strange thing: as soon as my opponent has had one let point called against him, he clears ten times better than before. Most of the time when he is in the way, he's doing it because he's a little tired and it requires too much effort to get out of the way. If he's penalized, then all of a sudden the game opens up and you can play squash."

Gamesmanship

There are all sorts of tricks that have been used on the
squash court to gain a psychological advantage. Reggie
Dumpshot, the quintessential gamesman, knew most of
them. He had refined squashmanship to a lethal art. One
of his ploys was to arrive late, hit one shot, and say, "I
have a train to catch, let's get this match over with." His
opponent wouldn't know that he had been warming up
for fifteen to twenty minutes on a nearby court.

Another trick of Dumpshot's was to take a couple of
frayed pieces of gut, weave them into a newly strung racquet, and place the racquet in his squash bag outside the
door of the court. At an appropriate moment he would
switch racquets, play a couple of quick points, and then
exclaim loudly over the "broken" strings. He refused to

switch back, however, and somehow he managed very crisp shots in spite of his equipment.

A favorite tactic Dumpshot used during play was to miss a volley intentionally and let the ball hit his opponent for an easy point, or if his opponent had already started to intercept the bogus volley, Dumpshot would drop back and hit an entirely different shot off the back wall.

Every one of these pieces of gamesmanship has been used in real matches. Only their perpetrator has been fabricated, in order to avoid libel. When I began this book, I hoped that my panel of experts would rally forth with plenty of Pottermanlike stories of ploys and counterplays, but I was to be disappointed. I was sure that Goldie Edwards, with her rich descriptions of the sport, would come through for me, but probe as I did, she would only say, "Gamesmanship is not part of my arsenal at all. I'm very direct and uncomplicated. There's a neurosurgeon I play with and we have fun, but if it's a match, I am serious and very straight."

The same with Niederhoffer: "I don't use gamesmanship. I don't believe in it. It's used on me. For example, many players believe they can upset their opponent's concentration through various nonsquash tactics. Sometimes when I am playing, my opponents will start out with the spin of the racquet. I will spin and they will walk over to see if I gave them a correct rough or smooth call. Or even before the spin, they might hit some fantastic shots or do a tremendous amount of running to give the symptom of great energy on their part. During the match itself there can be all sorts of states such as pretending to be extremely hostile, feigning injury, delaying the game, arguing with the referee, and pretending to be indifferent. When they do this, my opponents are just using up their own energies and admitting that they cannot win on squash alone."

My conclusion, after hearing the same story from each of my panel members, is this: the best players don't rely on gamesmanship, and they try to ignore it when it is used on them. Your opponent's state of mind, whether it be one of malice or guile, should be no concern of yours. You are usually being tested for susceptibility to distraction when these tricks are employed, and to pay attention to them is to surrender a part of your mind that should be working on the game.

The way to avoid being psyched *out* by your opponent is to arrive in a psyched-*up* condition yourself. You go on the court with positive thoughts as to your own ability and with a focus on the aspects of your game which you feel are going to be key in gaining victory. With this kind of attitude, and by paying attention to the singular importance of winning, attempts at gamesmanship by an opponent can only sharpen your will to win.

Reggie Dumpshot got his comeuppance one day when he pushed matters just a little too far. It seems that he was playing in a tournament at Merion Cricket Club against national champion Donald Strachan. Reggie was parking out in the middle of the court every time Don wanted to take a shot. And Don was having to call let or go around him. Reggie was taking advantage of the situation, and Don, who had quite a temper, finally had had enough, and yelled, "Dumpshot, if you don't get out of the middle of the court when I'm taking a shot, I'm gonna drive this ball right up your ass!"

There were women in the gallery, and so naturally everyone was quite shocked, and it was a very embarrassing moment. Play finally resumed, however. Strachan served, Dumpshot hit a medium speed ball back down the line, there followed several hard cross-courts until one by Dumpshot angled a little too sharply and came off the rear wall, and there he was, parked right on the T. Well, Strachan wound up and hit a devastating backhand right into the crease of Dumpshot's backside, and, amazingly, the ball stuck there for a full five or six seconds before it fell to the floor. No one could believe it. There was a gasp, followed by dead silence. Then, the entire gallery dissolved in laughter as Dumpshot stood there, red-faced and smarting-assed, having lost both his dignity and the point.

Babe Ruth would have been proud.

II
Prematch
Preparation

Conditioning for Endurance

In squash there is as much running as in soccer or basketball, but you cannot be substituted for. And it's much faster than tennis, with a lot less time between points. So if you want to play your best squash, you must be in good physical condition.

One of the reasons the Pakistanis have dominated squash is that they learned the game at high altitudes. Playing in thin air, they developed tremendous lung capacities. Hashim Khan is a good example of this. With his huge lungs and barrel chest, he can run all day on a squash court and never take a fast breath.

When I speak of conditioning, I am talking about the ability to endure one long point after another. In later sections, I will deal with ways of developing strength and speed.

There are two main types of cardiorespiratory exercises which will help build the endurance to carry you through long rallies: aerobic and anaerobic. You need some of both for the best results.

Aerobic exercises use energy derived from oxygen sources, so that you must be able to take in enough oxygen during the exercise to keep restoring the energy base. A 2-mile run is an ideal aerobic exercise. Jumping rope at a similar pace would also qualify, if you preferred that or could not get outdoors. Distance, jumping time, and frequencies would vary with age and the desired level of conditioning. Two to three times a week will maintain a good "club match" level of endurance.

Anaerobic exercises use energy which does not depend on the recovery of oxygen. If you run flat out up and down the squash court, as you must in some points, you will have used up all of your oxygen reserves, without restoring them, in as little as 35 to 40 seconds. Your legs ache, you are gasping for air, and you can't go on until you have replenished your oxygen. Wind sprints are good anaerobic exercises. Also good is speed-jumping or double-jumping with a jump rope, the latter being a double pass of the rope for each time you are airborne. The reason jumping rope is so good for squash players (as well as boxers) is that it makes you coordinate your arms and legs while giving both a good workout.

The six-point drill (Figure 2) is a special type of anaerobic conditioner for squash players. It takes ten to fifteen minutes and can be worked in after an easy match or following a practice session. You go on the court by yourself and start at the T with your racquet in the ready position as if you were waiting there for an opponent to return your deep rail shot.

Begin by moving in long, quick strides to the front left

Figure 2. The Six-Point Drill

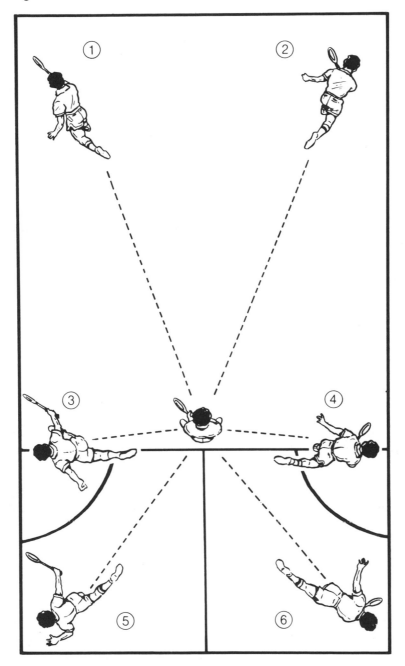

corner, stretch and hit an imaginary rail shot, rebound and backpedal in long steps to the T. Repeat to the front right corner and return to the T. Move laterally and hit a "volley," return to the T, and repeat on the opposite side. Go back into each corner and hit a "rail" or a "boast." Return to the T and start over at point number 1. Cover each numbered point three times for one set. This is a simulated point. Rest 30 seconds and repeat. A male college player in peak trim can do ten sets, 40 seconds each, with 30-second rest intervals. A forty-year-old businessman in good playing shape should be able to do six to eight sets, 50 seconds each, with 40-second rest intervals. Women's times would be about 5 to 10 seconds slower in each case.

Norm Peck says of his players, "What this means, if they can do ten hard sets, is that they can play ten very hard points consecutively. And most players cannot play ten straight hard points. In fact, I've yet to see a player who does not train in this manner who could play even three very hard points in a row. By hard points I mean points that are going to take you all over the court, that are going to last twenty-five to thirty shots."

For a mid-level player, the six-point drill is also an excellent way to develop "court presence," by being careful in terms of foot position, staying down on the shot, and executing a good stroke. It makes you determine and practice which foot to start with to arrive at proper stroking positions in the extremes of the court. If you are often late on your backswing, you should strive to feel the counterthrust of your racquet moving backward as your body moves forward. You should also try to reach each of the six points with as few steps as possible. Try to execute this drill in long, flowing strides.

In a sense, the six-point drill is similar to the *kata* exercise in karate, where emphasis is placed on developing perfect form and mental focus while fighting an imaginary opponent. This aspect of the six-point drill should not be slighted in the interest of cutting 3 to 5 seconds off the execution time.

A Program
for Squash Muscles

"In squash the single most important ingredient after skill is strength," says Goldie Edwards. "That's what's wrong with half of our women players. They can't even do push-ups—just lifting part of their own body weight.

"Look at the Aussie squash players, their women in particular, and see how strong they are compared to our squash players. The same was true of tennis fifteen years ago. They were beating us with regularity. Then Billie Jean King and Stan Smith found out how they were training, both for endurance and strength, and we turned it around.

"Getting a little stronger, getting that one extra thing going for you in addition to your skill, putting that **82** together with squash, improves the squash. The deep shots are stronger, the hard serve is stronger, the endurance is greater, you are quicker and faster.

"When you don't use your muscles, they start losing strength after about forty-eight hours. This happens at all ages, though it is more pronounced as you grow older. If you engage in a bout of exercise, or a bout of squash, or a bout of anything, you will get microscopic biochemical and physiological changes within your muscles. These changes will reverse themselves after about two days of inactivity. That's why most physical conditioning programs are done three days a week. That's why a football player at Pitt starts doing exercises the very next day after a knee operation. A guy in the street who doesn't know this or who doesn't have a doctor who knows about exercise, he's still limping around a year later.

"If you consider yourself an athlete, your musculoskeletal apparatus is your tool, and you have to pay attention to it and cultivate it in order for it to deliver its full potential."

When Goldie is not on a squash court, she teaches future teachers of physical education and conducts other college and graduate courses in tension control, health maintenance, and health improvement. On one of her sabbatical leaves she studied under Dr. Hans Kraus, specialist in physical medicine, world-renowned expert on muscle ailments and rehabilitation, and member of the President's Council on Physical Fitness and Sports. When I was researching this aspect of the game, I went to Dr. Kraus and asked him to help me develop an exercise program for squash muscles.

Dr. Kraus started by giving me a brief refresher course on the way muscles produce body movements. One muscle or muscle group contracts while an opposing muscle relaxes. For example, to bend your arm at the elbow, your biceps contract while your triceps relax, and to straighten it again the biceps relax while the triceps contract. If both sides of the muscle "team" are not co-operating, then the desired motion is impaired if not impossible.

Thus, a backswing, forehand, and follow-through depend just as much on the muscle's ability to give up contraction at the right time and in the right amount as they do on muscle strength. This aspect of flexibility enables the muscle to be strong through its full range of motion.

Loose, flexible muscles are so important to athletic performance and the avoidance of injury that you should begin any workout, practice, or match with relaxing and stretching exercises before even starting to warm up. For the best muscle condition you should also stretch and relax after cooling off from playing or exercising. I have constructed a mnemonic device for this routine called "Muscle Hill," shown in Figure 3.

Figure 3

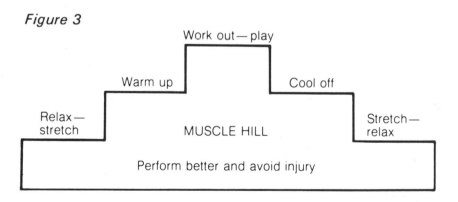

First, let's take the *stretching* exercises (Figure 4).

Dr. Kraus has recommended thirteen of these in the sequence shown. Each will stretch the muscles associated with one or more body joints. To get the best value from these exercises, it is important to stretch beyond the point of easy performance, to feel the pull in your muscles well past the range in which you normally use them. In fact, you should stretch until you are stopped by the mechanical limitations of your joints or the elasticity of your muscles. This does not mean that you should stretch violently or to the point of pain. Continual stretching over time will increase your range of movement in each joint and improve the flexibility of all these muscle groups. You will reap substantial benefits in your stroke production, reduced exposure to injury, and general well-being off the court.

Before getting into the frequency and duration of these exercises, let's look at their companion group of *strengthening* exercises (Figure 5).

The first fourteen of these fifteen use dumbbells, the last one, the weight of your own body. Once again, these exercises should be done in the sequence shown.

When lifting weights for strength, there is a generally held misconception, according to Dr. Kraus, that it is better to lift lighter weights more times than it is to lift heavier weights fewer times. Many people think that heavy weights produce tight muscles. This is not true. Tight muscles, as far as weight lifting is concerned, come from lifting too rapidly or from repeating the same exercise too many times without changing. Generally speaking, many repetitions with low weight increase endurance rather than strength. Only by lifting increasingly heavier weights will your muscles continue to get stronger.

The recommended approach to a weight-lifting workout is to begin by relaxing and stretching as before, and then, with a relatively light weight, do three or four of

Figure 4. Stretching for Squash

(Relax after each exercise, breathe deeply throughout)

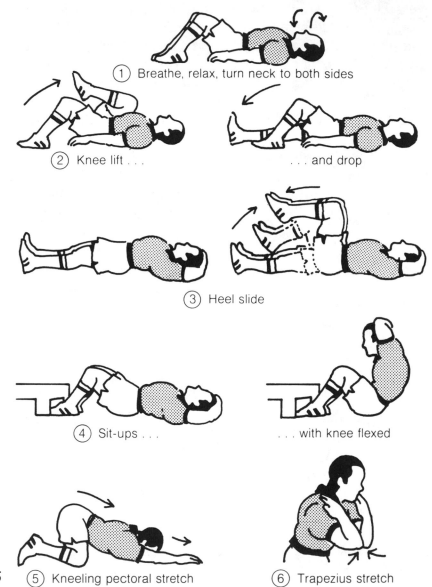

(1) Breathe, relax, turn neck to both sides

(2) Knee lift . . .   . . . and drop

(3) Heel slide

(4) Sit-ups . . .   . . . with knee flexed

86   (5) Kneeling pectoral stretch   (6) Trapezius stretch

⑦ Standing pectoral stretch

⑧ Soleus stretch

⑨ Calf muscle and Achilles stretch

⑩ Floor touch

⑪ Hamstring stretch

⑫ Groin-muscle stretch

⑬ Crossed hands, floor touch, and swivel—stretches everything

87

Figure 5. Strengthening for Squash

1 Curls

2 Reverse curls

3 Front elevations

4 Side elevations

5 Hands behind neck and back

6 Wrist curls and rolls

7 Bent-over one-arm rowing

88 8 Bent-over extensor lift

9 Hands across chest and out to side

10 Bent-over side lifts

11 Half knee-bends

12 Alternative overhead press

13 Full press

14 Bench press

15 Push-ups

89

each exercise, and go through the entire set of exercises; then start all over again with a heavier weight. Build up to your level of tolerance; then taper off with lighter and lighter weights until you are back where you started. Stretch your muscles, relax, and your weight-lifting workout is complete. You will have just climbed Muscle Hill.

It is important, when doing the stretching and strengthening exercises, to let go and relax, momentarily, after each one. The muscles need to "go loose" after each movement. By doing this, instead of keeping the muscles continually in a tensed state, you maintain the desired suppleness.

How do you use these two groups of exercises to help your squash game? What is the best program for your particular goals? If you are a thoroughly committed player, you will want to work them in along with your running, practicing, and playing. But because one person can do only so much, your program must be built around the rest of your life; it must be consistent with your other commitments and interests. I'll tell you how I manage my program, and you can work out your own.

About eight weeks or so before the winter leagues begin, I concentrate on weights and running. About four weeks ahead, I shift from recreational toward challenge ladder matches. At the same time I cut down on the amount of weight lifting and increase the solo practice sessions. After the season begins, I try to run twice a week, practice once or twice a week, and play every day except weekends. If I have an easy match one of those days, I will go into the weight room afterward and lift a few just to keep the muscles toned. And every day I try to do sit-ups and push-ups.

There are a few tricks you can use to help work these

exercises in. Dr. Kraus frowns on this, saying, "This is no substitute!" But then some stretching is better than no stretching. For example, if time is short when I'm headed to the courts, and I get stuck waiting for the elevator, I begin breathing and relaxing exercises. These can be done unobtrusively, so there is no embarrassment if others are nearby. If you're alone—if you have the good fortune to ride an empty elevator—you can begin limbering up as you go down. I lope to the club with long strides, continuing the deep breathing. I stretch the trapezius muscles while unbuttoning my shirt, and the hamstrings with the shoestrings. By the time I have dressed for play, I have pretty well gotten through the stretching exercises and can go right onto the court and begin warming up my strokes and the ball. This helps a lot if you play daily and yet must devote some time to earning a living. However, if I am playing an important match, I will try to allow enough time to do the entire routine very thoroughly before entering the court.

If you are an inactive person and are going to begin these exercises for the first time, it would be a good idea to base the working out of your program on the advice of your doctor. The main idea that should govern all these exercises is to work *gradually* up to your desired level of tolerance, whether that is the heaviest weight or the hardest cross-court drive.

I asked Dr. Kraus about other types of exercises and sports and their effect on squash. He thinks touch football and downhill skiing are not good for squash, mainly because of the high incidence of injuries in each. So if squash is your most important sport, you would do well to avoid those other two. He says isometric exercises, while they do strengthen, are not so good because they leave the muscles tight. A well-rounded gymnastics program would be good for squash. Swimming is good. Jogging is, of course, good. Cross-country skiing—because it strengthens arms, legs, and wind—is excellent. Other racquet sports are good.

Dr. Kraus is seventy-two. He exercises three times a week, using many of the routines he has recommended here. He chins by his fingers from the door lintel. He is a mountain climber. And he splits wood on weekends. I told him that the only muscle problems I had ever had in squash came from splitting wood on weekends.

"Tennis elbow?" he asked.

"Yes, and it lasted eight months."

"You've got to loosen, let go for a moment before striking again. And then, you probably were using a tool that was overweight, causing you to tense very much."

"Yes, I was."

"Well, what I do is split wood for a little while, then I saw, then I stack, then I saw, then I split. So. I keep changing the movements. Mix it up. Right?"

"Right!"

Practicing
the Basic Shots

"Ask Sharif Khan what sort of shots he's going to hit, what his game plan is, and he'll tell you 'I just play.' And that's how I do it. I don't think beyond the shot I'm hitting. My game is purely reflexive. The ball's here, it's in a certain position, and I hit the shot. I really don't know why I hit it. I've played a lot, I know the game, and it just happens."

Thank you, Peter Briggs.

For someone who has been hitting tennis and squash balls almost as long as he can remember, it is natural for him not to think of how and why he does it. As he said, his game has become reflexive. It is as if he had smart hands and they were doing the thinking and making the shots for him.

There is no secret to developing a reflexive game. You simply must hit enough rail shots so that you don't have to think about it when you hit one. And cross-courts, and reverse corners, and all the other shots that you want to perfect. There is only one way to do this: go on the court by yourself and practice the basic shots.

There are five basic squash shots you should practice:

Rail. The meat and potatoes of squash. This shot is aimed parallel and as close to either side wall as possible. It should bounce first at the service line and not be returnable off the rear wall. The rail shot is also known as an alley shot or a shot down the line.

Cross-court. The common alternative to hitting a rail shot. The cross-court is hit in a deep V from one side of the court to the other.

Roll corner. A shot usually hit from a few feet in front of the service line into the nearest side wall. The ball then angles to near the middle of the front wall, close to the tin, and should die short. This shot is also called a two-wall shot or, simply, a corner shot.

Reverse corner. This is one of the game's "exotic" shots, one which pleases galleries and seduces beginners. Although it is not hard to hit, it is usually hit at the wrong time. The reverse corner is hit across the body, from one side of the court, tight into an opposite corner, striking the side wall first.

Three-wall. This is another fancy shot usually hit from either rear corner sharp into the side wall. The ball angles to the opposite front corner, strikes the front wall, and often enough nicks (catches the wall and floor simultaneously and rolls out) on the side wall. Thus the shot is often called a three-wall nick. It is also called a boast, but some purists reserve this latter name for a three-wall shot which hits the opposite side wall *before* hitting the front wall, a difficult but absolutely killing shot if one can master it. Doug McLaggan, pro at Racquet and Tennis Club in New York, is said to have hit side-wall/side-wall/front-wall boasts at will in his salad days.

When you practice your shots, especially the rail shots, you are gaining that most important ingredient of good squash: control. Listen to Peter Briggs on the subject of control: "As you put the ball closer and closer to the wall, it takes away the angle; it cuts out a whole series of shots for your opponent.

"That's really the key aspect of control. When someone says, 'That player has control,' lots of people mistake that for meaning that the person being described can hit the ball right on a dime above the tin. Actually, that's good racquet work, whereas a player who really has control is one who from anywhere in the court can keep the ball at the right depth and right on the wall. I don't mean glued to the wall, but anywhere within two or three inches consistently. That is very, very hard to beat. Because, if you play like that, I don't care what kinds of shots your opponents have, they can't hit you."

"The best squash players," according to Cal Mac-Cracken, "do a lot of practicing by themselves. Mateer, Salaun, I used to do it. You take a ball, go in and go at it for an hour, and you come out absolutely dripping. You try all your shots. You set up certain routines, like hitting a reverse corner, so that you can hit them continuously without having to go chase the ball. You work out certain patterns just like a boxer who learns how to punch a punching bag. You learn certain exercises that approximate the speed and direction of the shot in the game, to help you get your timing and feel for the shot grooved into an automatic reflex."

Being away from squash for even short periods of time

can be frustrating because the motor coordinations required for finesse and control are easy to lose. "That's why I feel I have to hit a squash ball almost every day," says Goldie Edwards. "I can't afford for my timing to go. For maximal events, like running, throwing, or jumping, where gross strength is so important, it doesn't matter as much.

"I always like to warm up on my own at least twenty to thirty minutes before I play, and that is often my practice. Two shots require the greatest amount of control: rails and drops. So I usually practice those the most. When I practice drops—and I haven't seen anyone else practice this way—I actually drop the ball and do a half volley to get the feeling of the distance. I drop the ball with my left hand and with a half-cocked racquet I just sort of spoon it. I walk around and do this from different parts of the court. And then maybe I set up a few so I will get a moving ball. But if I have confidence with this little push-shot, half-volley thing, then usually it's going to work all right when we start playing."

There are three types of solo practice: single shots, combination shots, and random shots. All assume that you have learned the technical aspects of hitting the shot from a pro, coach, or very good player. Someone must show you where to make contact with the ball, where the follow-through should be, how much spin you should put on the ball, how hard you should hit, and so on. Once you know this, then you can begin practicing on your own.

So, let's say you are going to work on your roll corner, or side-wall/front-wall shot as some players call it (Figure 6). Pick the spot from which you are going to hit the shot, in this case 1 to 2 feet in front of the service line, or farther up, and from a foot to 5 feet away from the side wall. Then feed a ball up to the front wall that comes off of the side wall—not hard, something that you can work with—and hit the roll corner. Pick up the ball, hit it into the front wall so that it comes off the side wall, hit a roll corner. Pick up the ball . . .

And so it goes. Practicing comes easy to some; it helps if you enjoy a certain amount of solitude and if you are a bit of a perfectionist. Loving the game helps, too.

Figure 6. Roll-Corner Practice

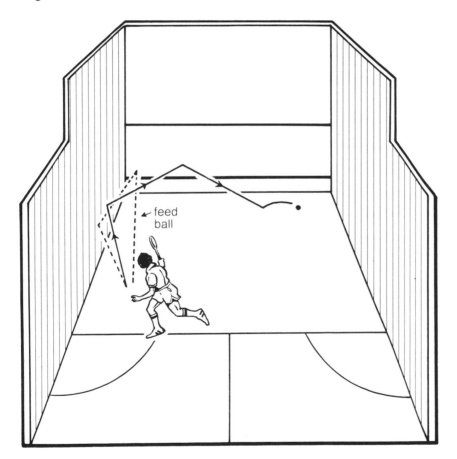

Two of the single-shot routines—the volley (Figure 7) and the reverse corner (Figure 8)—can be done in a continuous manner without stopping to pick up the ball. When you really get the ball going with these routines, they are actually a lot of fun.

Figure 7. Volleying Drill

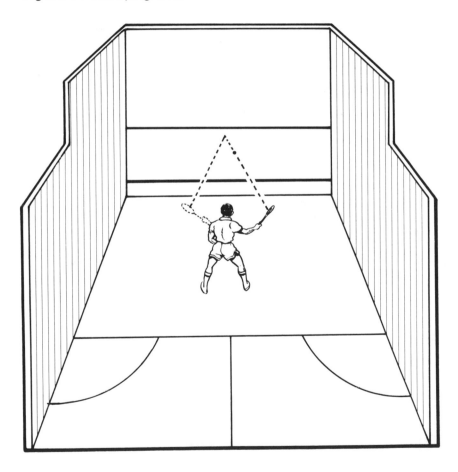

A good combination drill is the rail and three-wall shot (Figure 9). Very often in a game you will hit a rail. Suppose you hit it down the right-hand wall, your opponent hits another rail, and from the same spot from which you previously hit yours, and without changing your stance,

Figure 8. Reverse-Corner Drill

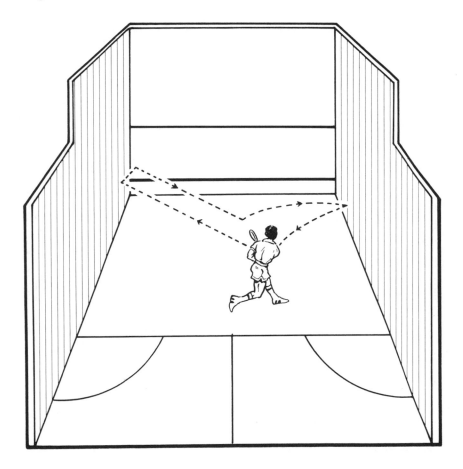

you go for the three-wall nick. A deadly combination. And very practiceable.

There are all sorts of drill possibilities a player can work out on his own to develop familiarity with the angles and speeds of the ball. Peter Briggs, when he is alone on the court, say between the third and fourth

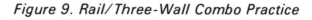

Figure 9. Rail/Three-Wall Combo Practice

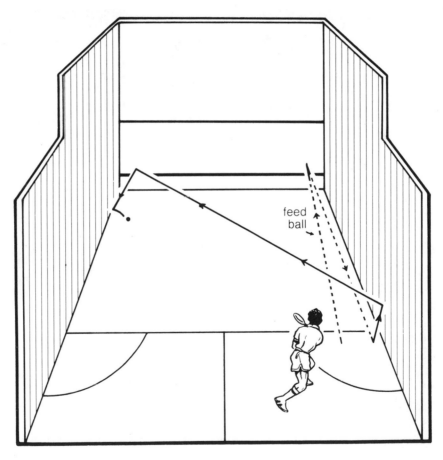

game, has a real gallery pleaser (Figure 10) which involves a backhand semilob followed by a backhand volley
reverse corner. The ball returns to the starting point,
where he throws up another semilob. There is an audible
sigh among the spectators when he goes into this little
number.

Figure 10. The Briggs Gallery Pleaser

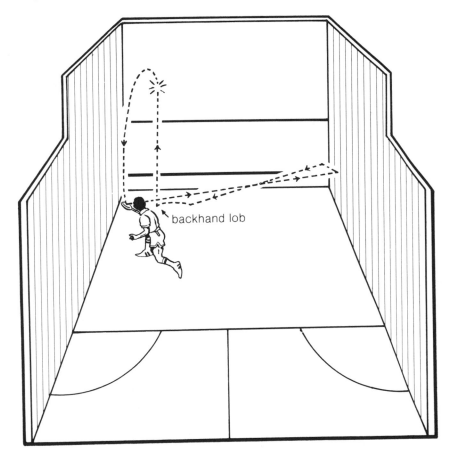

backhand lob

Vic Niederhoffer will sometimes warm up before an opponent comes on the court by making random shots—into the corners, small cross-courts, rails, and volleys—that cause him to twist and turn his body continually during the routine. He does this mainly as a way of getting his eye on the ball. Earlier in his career he used to play make-believe matches against himself, as did Hashim Khan when he was mastering the game. Playing against yourself requires consummate skill and conditioning and qualifies as the ultimate form of practice.

Target Shooting
with Rescigno

Rick Rescigno has devised a practice routine for the rail shot and the cross-court shot which he calls "target shooting." Rick says that ten hours of this routine can add three to five points to a mid-level player's game by helping him or her to groove the game's basic shots.

Let's take the rail shot first (Figure 11). On either the backhand or forehand rail shot, you should aim the first bounce at a rectangle which is centered on the service line and measures 1 foot by 4 feet. An absolute bull's-eye would be a first bounce on the service line as close to the side wall as possible without glancing off the side wall.

When your position on the court changes, the point of impact on the front wall changes, but your target always stays the same. The speed of the ball, likewise, would affect the height of impact on the front wall but not the **103** target. Therefore these targets are good for any type of ball such as the 70+ and the English balls. The four diagrams of Figure 11 showing various hitting positions (A to D) would apply to both forehand and backhand rail shots on both sides of the court.

An interesting way to target-shoot for rail shots is to play a game with yourself and keep score. You get

Figure 11. Position A

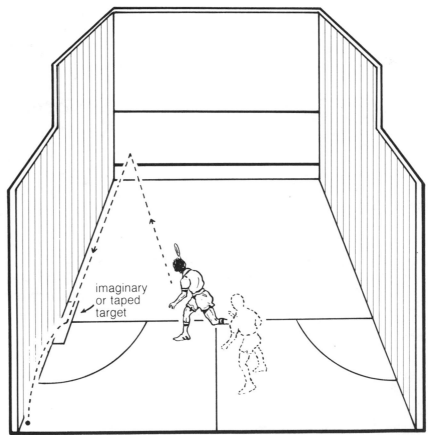

Target Shooting—Right-Handed Backhand Rail Shots

nothing for a ball that bounces outside the target, 1 point for a ball that hits the side wall *before* it bounces in the target, 2 points for a ball that hits the side wall *after* it bounces in the target, and 3 points for a ball that bounces in the target and bounces a second time without touching the side wall. That, sir, is a *clean* rail shot.

Pick a position to hit from, set up a moving ball, and hit

Figure 11. Position B

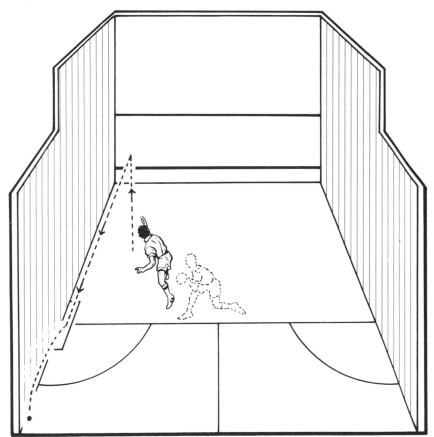

Target Shooting—Right-Handed Backhand Rail Shots

the rail shot. Note the score. Do this ten times on either forehand or backhand side. Score yourself according to this chart:

Rescigno's Rail-Shot Score Chart
0–10 pts.	Sub-par rails
11–20 pts.	Solid rails
21–30 pts.	Super rails

Figure 11. Position C

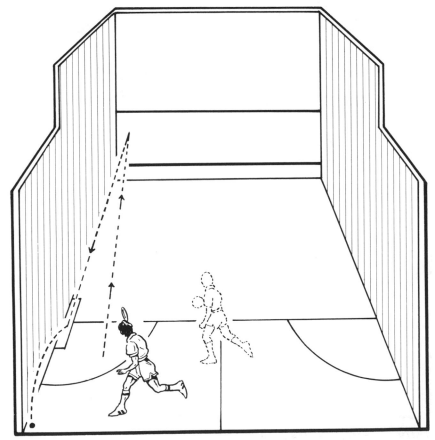

Target Shooting—Right-Handed Backhand Rail Shots

When target shooting, you may put down some masking tape to mark the target, but you will probably be better off if you don't, so that you train your eye to be target-conscious under game conditions. More advanced players can shrink the rail target to 6 inches wide by 2 feet long, still centered on the service line.

When practicing cross-courts (Figure 12), aim for a box on the side wall which starts at the service line and is 1

Figure 11. Position D

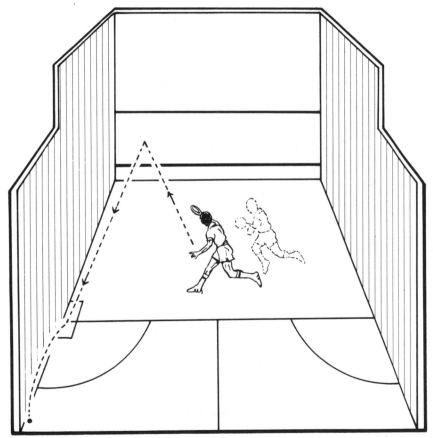

Target Shooting—Right-Handed Backhand Rail Shots

foot high and 4 feet long. This produces a shot which passes an opponent anywhere near the T at the farthest distance away and breaks off the side wall too low to bounce up for a get. It is a very effective shot. You may score yourself 1 point for a ball that hits the floor before the target and 2 points for one that hits the target on the fly. Accuracy on this shot is a little harder to achieve than

Figure 12. Position A

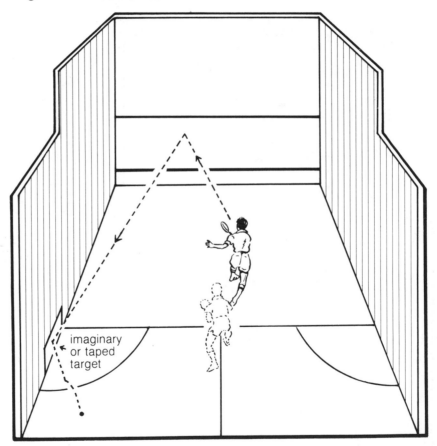

imaginary
or taped
target

Target Shooting—
Right-Handed Forehand Three-Quarter Cross-Courts

on the rail shot because of the wider variance in angles off the front wall. Score yourself according to this chart:

Rescigno's Cross-Court Score Chart

0–6 pts.	Sub-par cross-courts
7–13 pts.	Solid cross-courts
14–20 pts.	Super cross-courts

Figure 12. Position B

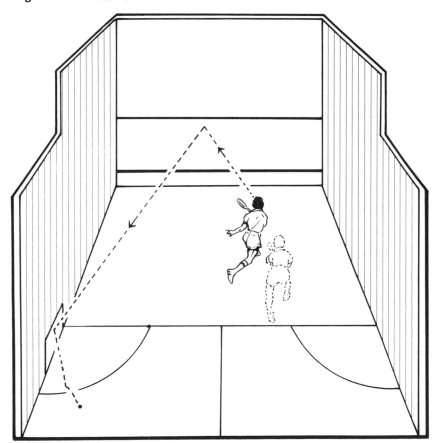

Target Shooting—
Right-Handed Forehand Three-Quarter Cross-Courts

When you have reached the point where you hit the rail and cross-court targets on both sides most of the time, you should also notice during actual play that formerly equal opponents are forced to hit more defensively and that you are being presented with a greater number of opportunities to make a putaway shot.

Figure 12. Position C

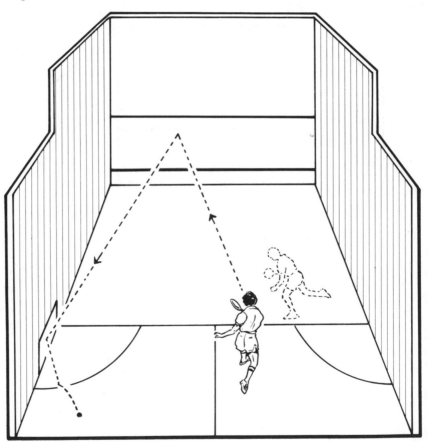

Target Shooting—
Right-Handed Forehand Three-Quarter Cross-Courts

One of the advantages of target shooting is that it simplifies your objectives for the game's basic shots. By doing this routine from various positions on the court, you will be learning to hit various spots on the front wall automatically to gain your desired result at the service boxes. In effect, the front wall will have become part of

Figure 12. Position D

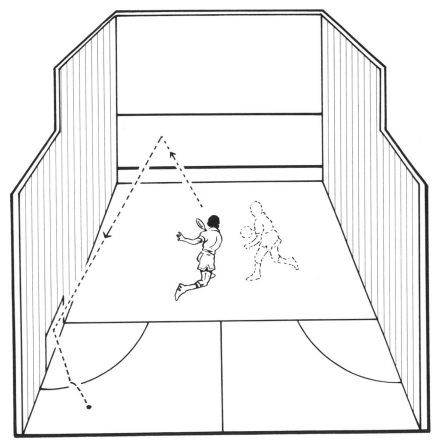

Target Shooting—
Right-Handed Forehand Three-Quarter Cross-Courts

your mental picture of the court, removing the temptation to look up from your shot to see where you want to hit the ball. And that, after all, is the point of target shooting.

Mental
Practice

"When I was learning squash, I did a lot of mental practicing," says Goldie Edwards. "I found the balls off the walls very difficult, and I didn't know which way to move. The ball would be going one way, I'd move toward it, and it would come off *into* me. So I began visualizing, between on-court sessions, what I was doing wrong, and I would picture myself making the correct move in the same situation. I can't *tell* you how much that helped. Now, over ten years later, I still use this technique to improve my stroking and shotmaking."

Mental practice is an old concept that is gaining popularity under such new names as "body thinking," and "visuomotor behavior rehearsal." Basically it consists of relaxing, screening out other stimuli, and rehearsing an **113** activity in the mind. A few years ago Jean-Claude Killy, while recovering from an injury, prepared for one of his races by skiing it mentally, and nothing more. The race turned out to be one of his best. More recently, mental practice has been used successfully by United States Olympic skiers and marksmen to prepare psychologically for their events.

The reason mental practice works can be demonstrated scientifically. In the context of squash, say that you decide to hit a backhand. A series of electrical impulses flows from your brain via motor nerves to the correct muscles, telling some to shorten and others to lengthen, which results in the basic movements for a backhand stroke. At the same time these impulses are on their way to the muscles, another part of the brain—call it the "shot memory"—compares its version of the backhand to where your arm, racquet, and the ball are, and sends signals to make last-minute adjustments to your stroke. The more you have practiced, the better picture you have of the stroke in your shot memory, and the better these last-minute adjustments are.

Take the problem many squash players have when receiving the serve. They wait with wrist cocked and the racquet in ideal position, but the grip is iron tight and *all* arm muscles are in advanced degrees of tension. In other words, the arm is rigid, as if momentarily set in concrete. Before the serve can be returned, they must cancel the signals which stiffen the arm and send out new ones for the appropriate service-return motions.

If these same players were to return serves in mental practice, with the goal of obtaining a firm grip and relaxed arm as they are waiting for the ball, and if electrodes were attached to measure the motor nerve impulses, they would in most cases experience a shift away from the electromyograph pattern for a tight arm to those for a loose arm. Repetitions of these mental rehearsals have been shown to strengthen and reinforce these nerve impulse patterns and in effect preprogram the nerve channels for the desired muscle action.

Thus, electromyographically, if you visualize a forehand, the bursts of nerve impulses are the same in microscopic form as if you were hitting the forehand.

So, once you know the stroke basics, you can begin practicing them mentally. As Goldie explains it, "First I try to be very relaxed, usually by sitting with my eyes closed. If you really understand the stroke, you can form a clear mental picture of it. Then I think my way through each phase of the stroke. I can see myself doing it, and I check the various reference points. I check the grip, the stance, shoulder position, where the racquet is on the backswing, position of the wrist and forearm, the ideal contact position, and the follow-through. I can actually visualize myself meeting the ball. The more times I do that the less I have to think about it on the court.

"In mental practice I think myself through a situation on the court. I go through the options. I visualize where the other person would be and choose the shot. Then I execute the shot, noticing the path of the ball as it fits the court.

"Some people never think about these things in between games. They wait and try to get it all together when they go on the court. I think you have to be *ahead* of the game, so when the situation arises, you are programmed and ready to go."

Niederhoffer's Notebook

We all like to examine the personal habits of a champion. We want to find out what makes him tick. Perhaps tucked away in his daily routine is a new key to winning.

Vic Niederhoffer is an ideal subject for this type of study. He likes to analyze his own routines to find out what variables have come together to produce the margin of victory on a given day. Or, if he lost, can he determine what bad influence entered, or what good measure was left out?

"I keep notes on my playing," he says. "I have a running tally on what I practice, my weight going in and coming out, the time I play, when and what I eat, how I feel when I'm playing, what lessons I've learned, what I can improve on.

116

"I have observed that successful people often keep good records. Systematic behavior and businesslike habits of organization have played a major part in my becoming a good squash player. I have always enjoyed keeping notes on quantitative things."

Here are selected entries from Niederhoffer's notebook. They are given in two sections: a diary-type record of his thoughts and observations upon leaving the court, and a tabular record of the more quantitative information.

6/6—Developed volley. Backhand volley on inside of ball has potential. Has right type of counter-clockwise spin to be good if hit into left side wall first. Trick on straight volley is to get it above tin. Forehand volley tins often. Crosscourt backhand volley has to nick to be good shot.

6/7—Wolf cracked under pressure. I'm not hitting enough shots. Volley was effective. Must work on return of hard serve. Sweating profusely. Court 75°.

6/8—Played three games with Wolf. Hit some good backhand reverse corners. Went for more shots. Was hitting lower. Volleyed a few. Served 2 double faults. String broke, ending play.

6/9—First day of vacation from daily practice in nine months. Getting soft.

6/10—Had self-doubts for 5 seconds after losing. Felt a little out of breath. Reverse corner bad. Footwork on stretch despicable. Drives not crisp enough. Goldstein volleying well. This is about the fourth time he beat me this year. Must learn to keep the wolf out of the door in the fall, rather than having to grab him by the claws and fangs and throw him out in the winter.

6/12—Forehand reverse corner. First time it ever worked. Hit it flat, with sidearm motion. Finally it stays off tin. Strategy awareness: each shot should be hit for a possible point winner. Of course, this is opposite of how I usually

				Exercises			
Date	*Time In–Out/Weight In–Out*	*S/U*	*P/U*	*Hops*	*Sprints[1]*	*Food[2]*
6/6/75	8:40–10:20/190 189	10	35	100	20	BS-11:00-1C/2P BP-6:30-2C/1P
6/7	7:10–9:00/191–188	10	30	100	15	BS-10:00-2P BP-1:30-2C
6/8	8:00–9:15/190–188.5	10	20	—	15	BS-10:30-2C/2P BP-3:30-2C/1P
6/10	9:00–9:40/191–189	15	38	150	18	BS-11:00-1C/2P BP-6:30-2C
6/12	9:00–10:30/190.5–188	12	30	140	20	BS-11:00-2C/2P BP-4:00-3C
6/13	8:30–9:10/191–188.5	—	25	didn't do sprints home—getting soft		BS-10:30-2P BP-2:30-2C/1P
6/14	4:30–5:20/191–189	14	36	160	15	BS-10:00-2P/1C BP-1:00-2C
6/15	10:30–11:10/192–189	15	37	160	—	BS-10:00-2P BP-6:30-2C/1P
6/16	8:35–9:05/192.5–190.5	—	—	—	20	BS-9:45-2P/1C BP-4:30-2C
6/17	8:20–9:30/191.5–188.5	18	41	150	15	BS-11:00-2P/2C BP-5:30-2C/1P
6/18	8:30–9:45/190–191	16	40	150	20	BS-10:30-2P/1C BP-6:00-2C
6/19	8:00–9:00/192–189	15	40	140	15	BS-11:00-2P/2C BP-5:00-2C/1P

[1] Sprints = no. of city blocks.
[2] BS = before sleep; BP = before play; C = carbohydrate portion; P = protein portion.
[3] P = poor; M = medium; G = good.

118

Quality of Sleep	Quality of Business Day	Opponent/Score/Quality of Play
1:00–9:30 P[3]	M[3]	Mir/15-10, 15-12, 12-15, 15-14/G[3]
1:00–9:30/M	M	Wolf/15-10, 14-15, 15-14, 18-14/G
1:15–9:00/G	G	Wolf/15-10, 15-5, 15-5/G
1:30–9:00/P	M	Goldstein/10-15, 8-15, 8-15/P
1:45–8:30/M	G	Mir/12-15, 15-11, 15-10, 15-12/M
2:00–9:01/P	M	Goldstein/15-12, 12-15, 15-12, 15-4/M
1:00–9:00/P	M	Practice alone
2:00–9:00/G	M	Greenberg/12-15, 14-17, 9-15, 12-15/P
1:35–8:35/G	P	Mir/15-10, 13-15, 15-11, 15-12/G
1:30–8:30/M	M	Greenberg/15-8, 15-12, 10-15, 18-17/G
2:00–8:00/M	G	Mir/10-15, 8-15, 18-16, 12-15/P
1:30–8:30/G	M	Practice alone

play but it's something to try nevertheless. Must run more for crotch shots. Tendency too much to let them go in practice.

6/13—Beginning to hit more shots. Reverse corner worked. Tried work on reverse corner off same swing as cross-court drop. Starting to hit hard and deep. Many long points. Was floating on clouds of victory.

6/14—Backhand 3-wall nick. It must be hit without picking up arm. This keeps it near nick on side wall. To get backhand 3-wall nick onto right side wall first, hit up on inside of ball. One of the first worthwhile practices I've had. And gave little Galt a lesson albeit I also fussed at her.

6/15—Worked on cross-court shot, trying not to hit the side wall. Must put more outside spin on ball to keep it off. Body not moving very well. Was using new racquet. One of the worst losses ever. Felt pain in stomach when we started. Incredibly small margin between winning and losing. Sow the wind, reap the whirlwind. Am I getting old? Greenberg almost knocked me over.

6/16—Broke in new racquet. Began to move better. Worked on forehand straight drop. Deception must be mixed in with correct angle. No gain without pain. Every time I hit blister hurt. Developing systematic spin table for both sides of court. Gail called to say match with Khan is off. The beaver builds his dam, and just as it is ready, it is washed away. So the beaver begins over again.

6/17—Played errorless squash. Good deceptive mix with reverse corner. Forehand cross-court drop of interest. Must be hit close to body, almost from belly button. Volley must be hit with margin. Does have potential as an offensive shot if it clears tin by good margin. A whole new concept of completely offensive game. Could revolutionize the game. A switch from my safe game of 74–75.

6/18—Lost 3/1 to Mir. Received terrible drubbing. Didn't keep it to the backhand. Felt okay, but wasn't moving well.

Managed to gain a pound in an hour and fifteen minutes. Thought about business entire time. Tried overhead 3-wall nicks. Not enough power. Hardly worked up a sweat.

6/19—Play consisted mainly of practice of forehand reverse corner. Finally began to get touch. Must get under ball, as well as turn grip. Callus started to act up. Was doing my exercises at 9:00 when along came night watchman to turn off lights, throwing me into pitch darkness. I was back in the Pit and the Pendulum. The four walls were slowly compressing. What a fright. What an experience. Few have known a squash court like me and yet I was lost. The night watchman was going to do me in like my janitor had murdered my monkey many years earlier in Chicago. I couldn't see. I sweated with agony. I felt along the wall, looking for the door. Couldn't find it. I was on the side wall. Looked on the back wall for the door. Then I felt it but couldn't get out. Dumb me. Tried for five minutes to get out, fooling with the latch. Gradually the fear let go of me. I fortunately was on Court 8 at the Harvard Club which has an open gallery. Plenty of push-ups finally came in handy. I jumped, grabbed, and I was free. The only time a player should be alone on a squash court with the lights turned off is with a voluptuous broad.

6/20—Developed a number of ideas. Backhand reverse corner seems to bounce well when I keep the racquet in close to the knees. Forehand straight drop appears to be more deceptive when I rotate body to right like a rubber-band. Forehand cross-court drop shot must have good margin.

6/21—Very bad day. Didn't play. Took wrong racquet to courts. Read 2 books on squash instead. Similarity in evolution—squash tennis once bigger than racquetball?

6/22—Played well: How come? Was it that I didn't play on 6/21? Was it two-hour rest before playing? Must quantify. Will not achieve greatness if I continue to be unsystematic.

6/23—Practiced rudiments only. No fire in legs. Need better motivation. Hard backhand is something I've never had. Must practice this again. What is secret of why the further you are from the ball the harder you can hit the shot? Watch angle of the hard serve more.

6/24—Developed a new concept. On backhand keep racquet head going forward rather than arm. Hit it like a fly swatter. Sort of like Ufford does. Also developed idea of forehand reverse corner mixed up with backhand cross-court. I've got to move well to make this work.

Game
Diagraming

Because of the varied and strategic nature of the game, squash lends itself to a diagrammatic analysis for the purpose of studying the strengths and weaknesses of a given player. The results of this analysis in turn can be used to help the analyzed player improve his or her game. Or it can be used in an upcoming match to help defeat the analyzed player.

There are two different methods of diagraming: one which records the errors and winners of a player, another which records the end sequence of shots in a point. I will explain each and discuss its merits.

Suppose that you are going to play Nick Boast in an upcoming club tournament and you need all the help you can get. A week or two before your match you go into the gallery and analyze his game.

In the first method, using a diagram of the court and coded symbols, you record Boast's winners and errors, noting the location and type of shot he selected for each. Your diagram for one game might look like Figure 13. Arrows show the direction in which the ball is being hit. A circle around a symbol indicates an error; an uncircled symbol is a winner. And here is the code, which you will need in order to diagram by either method:

r = rail shot	v = volley
cc = cross-court	½v = half volley
2w = 2-wall (roll corner)	s = serve
3w = 3-wall (boast)	hs = hard serve
rc = reverse corner	n = nick
d = drop shot	f = forehand
l = lob	b = backhand

Counting up the shots of Boast's game shown in Figure 13, you get ten winners and four errors (circled). From this you conclude that Boast's opponent made five errors in order for Boast to reach his score of 15. You could have kept a separate diagram for his opponent, but squash is fast and it takes time to learn what to watch and how to code the shots. You're mainly interested in Boast's game anyway.

So, looking at the diagram of Boast's first game, you conclude that he tends to hit down the line off his backhand and, unless kept deep on that side, is dangerous. His forehand volley is versatile. With it he hit a reverse corner, a cross-court, and a rail—all winners. About the only weakness seems to be his forehand in the rear court.

Using this approach and diagraming several of Boast's games, if possible against different opponents, you emerge with the basis for a game plan in your own match

Figure 13

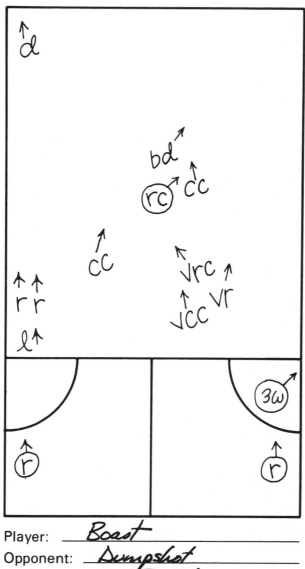

Player: *Boast*

Opponent: *Dumpshot*

Racquet Hand: *Right*

Score: *15/11*

with him. If he sees you taking notes in the gallery, it may or may not bother him, but it isn't likely to increase his confidence when he plays you.

Let's take a look at some more game diagrams and their interpretations. In Figure 14, we have a transplanted English player using the 70+ ball, which has characteristics similar to the English ball. You will note the great number of two-wall shots hit from the rear court. There were also fourteen winners, indicating good control on the part of both players in that all but one point was earned by the winner. To keep this player from hitting his favorite shot, one would have to use high lobs, keep the ball very tight to the wall, or be very effective with touch shots up front.

Figure 15 shows a game where the winner made seven errors and the loser, six. Three of the winner's errors were volley reverse-corners, a questionable choice from that position. Also, note that this player hit two forehands from his backhand side. Apparently, the loser was aware of this conceptual weak spot and was taking good advantage by aiming a lot of his shots into that zone. This diagram, which records a most unusual game, shows the analytical potential of the game diagraming technique. With so coherent a picture of a player's shooting habits, you could develop a very specific strategy to use against him.

The second method of diagraming shows the last two or three shots of a point. It overcomes the main criticism of the first method: showing winners and errors out of context doesn't tell you what shots led up to the winner or error. And very often the setup is even more important than the finishing shot.

For example, in Figure 16, Nick Boast hit a three-quarter cross-court, his opponent hit a three-wall shot,

Figure 14

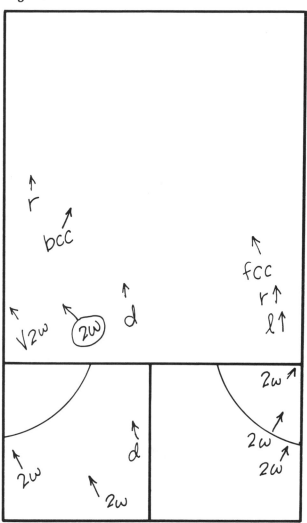

Player: _Hyder_
Opponent: _Leathers_
Racquet Hand _Right_
Score: _15/10_

Figure 15

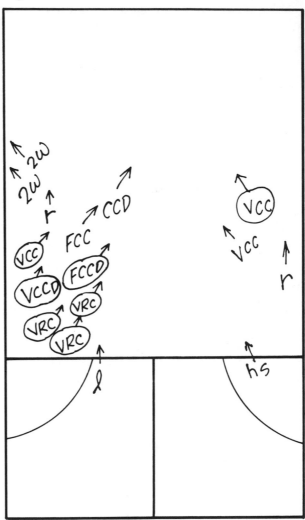

Player: _Shirdasani_

Opponent: _Hollingshead_

Racquet Hand: _Right_

Score: _15/14_

Figure 16

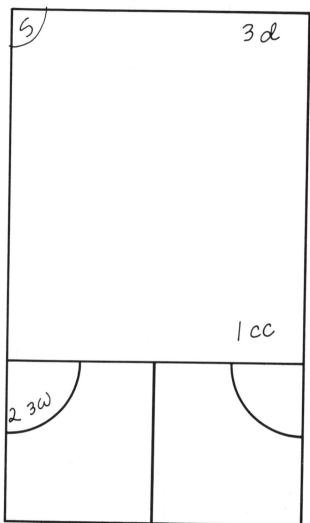

and Nick went up for the winner on a drop shot. The S in the corner tells you it was a short point. There may have been additional shots during the point, but they are not included if not key to the "terminal exchange."

In Figure 17, a medium-length point, Nick hits a rail,

Figure 17

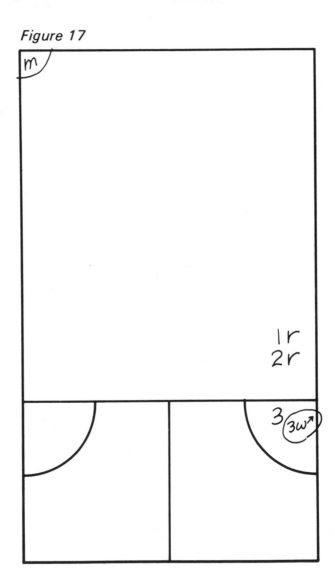

his opponent returns a rail, and Nick misses with a three-wall shot.

In Figure 18, Nick was forced deep to his backhand corner with a cross-court after he had hit a rail shot. He tried a rail down the left and missed.

Figure 18

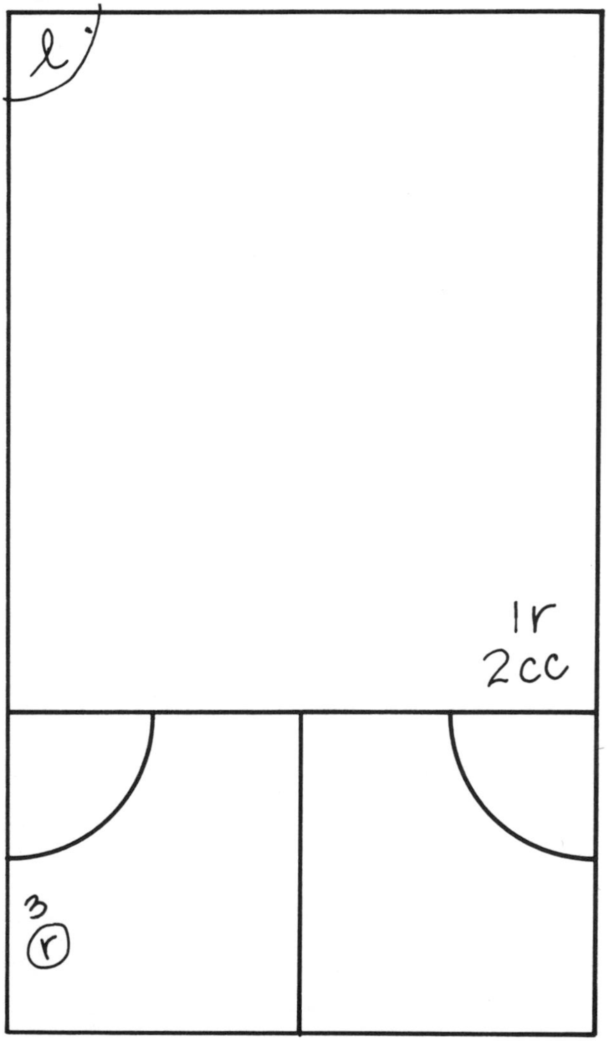

You figure that since you are only interested in Boast's game, all points you diagram end on his shot, and therefore you only need the sequence to know which player hit what shot.

What to Eat Before a Match

If you have a big match coming up, how soon do you start paying attention to how much and what type of food is in your body? When, in effect, do you go on a "match diet?"

Vic Niederhoffer likes to have meat eight or nine hours ahead and a lot of carbohydrates such as mashed potatoes, spaghetti, or bread a few hours before he plays. Between two matches on the same day he sticks mainly with juices and carbohydrates.

Norm Peck agrees with the carbohydrates as the main ingredient of your last meal before a match. He advises the Princeton players to eat pancakes two to three hours beforehand because they seem to give more residual benefits than other starches.

You should know the following facts as a background **133**

for understanding your needs for certain foods. First, the physical demands of squash deplete your body's stores of sugar, salt, water, and other substances. These need to be replaced in varying amounts and intervals, depending on the degree of depletion and your playing schedule.

Carbohydrates turn into glucose (body sugar) when digested. Glucose is converted into glycogen, which is stored in your liver and muscles. Glycogen is the body's basic muscle fuel. There is normally enough glycogen in your cells to fuel about three hours of squash, so the average player doesn't have to worry. But, for two matches in one day, or for top-level marathon rallies, a player must replace the glycogen stores. Fructose, or fruit sugar, as found especially in honey, and to a lesser extent in fruit juices, promotes a rapid replacement of depleted glycogen reserves.

There is a training technique known as *glycogen boosting* which can be useful to players who regularly get into long, hard matches. Taking advantage of this technique involves three steps: first, you exhaust your glycogen reserves with a particularly long match or other type of workout, usually accompanied by a lot of sweating. Then you eat only proteins and fats for two or three days. Finally, you eat mainly carbohydrates for two or three days. At this point your glycogen level should be nearly double its normal level, and you are ready for the "big match." Remember, though, that glycogen boosting isn't really needed at less than the highest tournament levels.

Replacing salt is most effectively confined to using it on your food. However, if you are playing in hot courts, or otherwise lose an unusual amount of water during a match, you may also wish to use one of the electrolyte drinks during or right after a hard match to replace lost sugar, salt, magnesium, potassium, and water. Salt tablets are no longer accepted as the best way to replace lost salt. Vitamin C has come back into favor as a strengthener of the immune response to upper respiratory infections. And women players should add some form of iron supplement on a regular basis.

For women squash players, Goldie Edwards says that there is no need to overload on carbohydrates. "Very few women's matches last longer than an hour," she says. "Now I feel good if I've had some carbohydrates, but if I've had too much, my mouth gets dry. And I feel thirsty. That's because carbohydrates actually absorb fluid from the tissues. So if I'm going to have carbohydrates, I just make sure there's not too much."

At a tournament, you often have to eat what's available, what they are serving. Goldie tries to stay away from fat. "I try to keep away too from things like lettuce and cabbage, things that might be gas-forming in the intestines. I'll go for rolls. Very often at these tournament luncheons they serve chicken in some form, and that I usually find fine. If there's a nice ripe banana around, I eat that. I drink tea or coffee. Strangely, if the coffee is decaffeinated, I get a headache.

"Chocolate bars, you know, are high fat. And they make you very thirsty. The other thing is, people who drink Cokes and eat a lot of candy bars before they play can induce what is tantamount to insulin shock in themselves. It works this way. You drink maybe a couple of Cokes and then you go on and play, and about twenty minutes into the game, you get a weakness, and you feel a bit jittery. What happens, you see, is that you bump up the blood sugar level very high with this sucrose, with this sugar in the Coke, and you feel really good for a little while, and then the pancreas comes along with an outpouring of insulin, and the insulin takes out the blood sugar, which it is supposed to do, but you have overstimulated the pancreas. So you produce a lot of insulin, and it really lowers the blood glucose level to below what it was, and if you're not careful it can put you in the hypoglycemic range, and that's when you feel the dizziness and weakness. That will pass when you mobilize your own stores to right it again. It's something that various people are sensitive to, and they can never understand why this has happened."

III
Match
Play

Warming Up

What do you do during the warmup before a match? Can you gain valuable prematch intelligence? How do you go about sizing up your opponent? Here is what Briggs, Edwards, MacCracken, and Peck have to say:

Peter Briggs: "It is totally impossible to learn from a guy by watching him warm up. There are guys who have never lost a warmup in their life! There are other guys who will purposely look weak on a particular stroke when actually they're not.

"What you are really doing in a warming up is personally trying to get loose, get your eye on the ball. It's all personal.

"I usually hit the ball back to the guy rather than take six or eight forehands in a row. But I don't play until I'm ready to play. If he's ready and I'm not, and I need to hit **139** thirty balls down the rail by myself, I'll do it. I don't care what he thinks."

Goldie Edwards: "Sometimes if I haven't seen my opponent before and it's a match, I will try to put on a show in the warmup. I hit hard a lot and try to make an impression on them. I try to hit good-length balls that get the nick and see how they deal with that.

"You get some players who will hit six to themselves and then hit one to you. I think that's not fair. I think you've got to watch this person carefully. Perhaps they might not be fair when it comes to something more significant. So you've got to watch the score, watch if all the balls are up, you know, watch them like a hawk.

"I watch my opponents to see if they let the ball bounce twice in the warmup. If they do then I know they are going to be a little bit slow and laissez-faire during the game. Barbara Maltby would never let a ball bounce twice in a warmup. She knows better than that. You see, you have to get the ball on the one-bounce in the game, and the warmup is the warmup for the game. And yet some players regularly let the ball bounce twice. Now they're the ones who aren't going to get to the top. They're just not going to do it. Because that's their whole approach to competitive squash, and it just isn't enough."

Cal MacCracken: "Warmups don't have to be those back-and-forth cross-courts to each other all the time, where you concentrate on your own shots. They can have much more purpose. You don't have to give your opponents the same shot every time. You can certainly watch how they hit a backhand versus a forehand, how they hit low versus high shots, how they hit a shot that breaks off the wall, and whether they can pick it off close to the side wall. Then you will be able to plan your game based on their weaknesses."

Norm Peck: "The first thing we tell our players is to avoid generalities based on opponent's physical makeup. You know, if a player is six feet three and two hundred pounds, the obvious generality is that he hits the ball hard and is somewhat clumsy. Or if the player is five-six and a hundred and thirty-five pounds, that he scrambles around and uses a lot of junk shots. But the stereotype doesn't always work. For example, Arif Sarfraz, who is very small, can hit the ball harder than most big players. And Frank Brosens, who is very large, has more touch than most players on our team.

"There *are* some things you can look for in the warmup that can be helpful. For example, a player who warms up intelligently will oftentimes be a well-coached and fairly intelligent player. He takes his time, hits the ball softly at the beginning, keeps the ball off the tin, and just gets used to the feel of the ball and how it reacts on the court, particularly if it's a strange court. This type of player is likely to hit some smart shots during the course of a match.

"On the other hand, a player who goes into the warmup and hits the first shot as hard as he can, and all he really does is kind of bang the ball around, hits a lot of tins, hits the ball kind of flat, this type of player will usually play the same kind of game. We have a standing joke that he's warming up his tin shots.

"One of the things we tell each of our players to do, particularly if we are playing an away match and have driven three hours or so, is to go on the court a half hour to forty-five minutes before the match, to hit for fifteen or twenty minutes alone, to really work on his shots, get himself loose, and prepare himself mentally for the match he is about to play."

Choosing
a Game Plan

Squash has been described as physical chess. A game wherein you move opponents around the court with a pre-planned series of shots until they are in a weak enough position for you to hit an easy winner.

The chess analogy is apt only up to a point. In squash, instead of a reflective pause between shots, there is a constant interaction between the physical and the mental, and there is no finite number of responses to a shot. In effect, preplanning or strategy can be a some-time thing. It may work during one part of the game and fail at another.

"Consider for a moment what happens in the course of a point," says Norm Peck. "Most players—I'd say ninety-five percent of all the people I've seen play squash—are very predictable in what they do. They will **142** hit the same shot off a given shot just about every time they get it. For example, if I were to hit you a three-wall shot, you will most likely go up and return it cross-court. So I hit that three-wall, and then I can move only halfway back to the T and wait for your cross-court. Then I can just lay that ball back down the line. And if you're not thinking about what you are doing, I'll do this to you all day, and you won't realize it, you really won't.

"Or, say that I hit a ball deep to your forehand corner. Most players are taught in the beginning to hit a rail shot if the ball is in the back court. So I hit one into that corner and then I just kind of slide over a half step or so, nothing dramatic, and as soon as the ball leaves your racquet, I take the other half step and cut that rail shot of yours off. And, again, I'll do this over and over, until something goes on in your head that says, 'Maybe I'd better hit cross-court.' So you will surprise me with the first cross-court. But the next time you do that, you'll say, 'The cross-court worked—I'll hit cross-courts off his rails,' and you hit me three, four, five of them, and I'll cut off the next four.

"So it's really a game where you have to be *mentally* a step ahead of the other player."

A game plan should not be too elaborate. It ought to be flexible, permitting you to adjust as play progresses. "The average player should have a few shots he can win points with," says Vic Niederhoffer. "He should vary the frequency with which he tries to hit these shots during the match. Depending on how tired and how well his opponent is playing, he should change the game dynamics and vary the risk/reward ratio."

Peter Briggs avoids picking a game plan until after he has played the first game. "Once you have played him a game, you can pretty much tell: Does the guy move up and back well? Does he volley the ball? How hard does he hit the ball? How close to the tin does he hit the ball?

"Lots of guys are great shooters, but they go very close to the tin, so the way to play them is to keep the ball in play. Sooner or later, they'll just get frustrated and miss.

"There are other guys who have long, fluid strokes, so you volley everything you can get ahold of, and you try to rush them. And if the guy is tall, you try *not* to put him in a position where he will use his reach. Try instead to keep him tangled up in his long arms."

Let's extend Peter Briggs's approach to the type of player you often meet at the beginning levels of league play: the hard hitter who has learned how to hit ground strokes and loves the visceral surge to be derived from sizzling rails and cross-courts. These players usually do not stroke well above the shoulder level, so the thing to do is keep the ball out of their groove with shots that require volleying.

Another approach to playing ahead is to understand that there are certain shots which will bring a somewhat predictable response. Norm Peck gives a good example of this: "If I hit a forcing cross-court to the left which breaks off behind you, there are only a few things you can do with the ball from back there. You've got to use the side wall to get that ball up to the front court, and I know it's going to end up in the right front court.

"So as soon as I have hit that shot, I'm paying attention to what you're doing. I've watched you use the side wall and I'm moving up and over even as the ball passes me going to the front wall. So I'm there waiting when the ball arrives, and I can usually just dump it in the right front corner for an easy point."

It can be useful to think of a player who effectively uses a game plan as having passed the Exotic Shot/Fat Ball course at Squash College. That is, before you can hope to employ strategy and select shots under pressure, you must have gone through this famous school, whose small white campuses are located all over the country. Listen to Professor Niederhoffer, one of the visiting lecturers:

"The problem of going for exotic shots is a very common one. It is probably the biggest weakness that elementary competitive players have. As in all things, the key to this problem is preparation. Ninety-nine percent of hitting the right shot is being prepared to do so.

"Most times when players hit an exotic shot they are out of position or are desperate to conserve energy. If your opponents can get to the shot, they are going to make a point on it, plus you're generally going to miss the shot, and furthermore it's just not an effective strategic time to do it.

"One of the worst things in shots is to lean back and hit them with a loft. All the shots have to be hit, like drives, with a tremendous margin of error, and you can only do this if you're leaning forward and you're in good position to hit it.

"And what about the player who gives in to the impulse to pulverize a fat ball? Well, I will simply state that the desire to release tension or end points quickly is antithetical to the complete squash player. When a setup occurs, instead of looking at it as the *end* of a point, you should think of this fat ball as the *beginning* of the end, the prelude to a series of shots which should lead to a position where ultimately you will be able to hit the one shot that gives you a reasonable chance of a winner and almost no chance of a loser. Only then do you try to end the point.

"The whole question of success in developing a game plan, of being capable of understanding and using the strategies of squash, is resolved in your mental attitude toward the game. Are you patient? Do you pay attention to detail? Do you have respect for your own abilities to keep going? If you have these qualities, you have a chance to be a very good player."

Controlling Your Mind on the Court

This is a very personal topic and a very personal moment as I write about it. I have just come from a city "D" singles match that went to five games, three of which were overtime. I was leading 11-7 in the fifth, and I guess I thought the match was in the bag. But it wasn't.

Again, I remember last fall when we took our club players down to play the undergraduates at Princeton. After my regular match, I played a pickup game with Nancy Gengler, then the women's intercollegiate champion and stalwart, along with Amy Knox, of the Princeton women's team. We were both playing well, I with some forcing cross-courts and rails, she with some beautiful gets and touch shots, and then we arrived at 13-all.

Nancy chose five-out-of-nine as a tiebreaker. On the next

point we got into an extended rally until she hit a deep ball that broke off the right wall and came off the back wall slightly to the left of center. I backed up on it and really whanged one—right into her fanny.

Until that moment the sex thing had not entered my head. But there I stood, feeling awful and thinking of the round red mark with the small white center welling up there under the shorts of this fragile Princeton coed. We played a let and Nancy proceeded to win the next five points and the game.

What can happen to an athlete's mind in mid-contest is only magnified in the game of squash. In terms of the time available to react, position, and stroke, it is the fastest of racquet sports, with the added challenge of contending with another body for the same space. All these characteristics place a huge premium on the ability to maintain concentration.

You are there, in the confines of a small white room. The ball is streaking up and down the rails. You move to the T, retreat to the corner, squeeze around your opponent and go back to the T. "That's why the game is so unique," says Peter Briggs. "It's like boxing because of its closeness and intensity. Both players are physically contained. There's nowhere to go. You can look anywhere you want and all you see is walls or the other guy. Or the gallery. And there's no solace from the gallery, because they're just a sea of faces staring down at you."

To counteract this intensity and confinement, Peter tries to maintain a sense of detachment during a match. "If anything," he says, "I would tend to keep a very good humor on the court. Maybe crack a couple of jokes. I do this, because in the end you have to keep things in perspective. You've got to realize basically the total inaneness of what you are doing. Scurrying around in a white room chasing a small black ball. I'm fully aware of that all the time. That's why I can go into the court and, whether I win or lose, I forget about it once I'm out of the court. I find a guy who takes this totally seriously a little bit amusing. Everything, even the most serious squash match, needs tempering."

So you learn to do it for yourself, to stay even-tempered, to hold off distractions, to play at your level best throughout the match. How you do this is, again, a very personal matter, subject to great variation, both among individual players and from match to match.

The year that all four semifinalists at the women's national intercollegiates were Princetonians, Betty Constable's players were termed "ice goddesses" by the press because of their steely powers of concentration. She had taught them: "None of this gallery stuff. *Never* look in the gallery. It's too distracting. The moment you look in the gallery your concentration goes. You've got a lot of work to do in that court. The only person you ever look at is the referee, to ask for a let. Once you look beyond and see a friend or someone else, you've lost two points. How're you going to get your mind back? The game's too fast."

Cal MacCracken's approach is to concentrate on his opponent's weakness. "If you will analytically try to study what the other person's weakness is, then you concentrate on that and forget your own problems and errors. You do two things this way: you obviously improve because you do better if you continually press opponents by hitting to their weakness, but the main thing is that you take your mind off yourself, and that usually overcomes panic."

Cal also tells how you can be distracted by an opponent's injury. He recalls the time he was playing Henri

Salaun, and Salaun twisted his knee. "He lay on his back moaning. After I had won the first two games and was leading him ten to three in the third. I really thought he would never walk again. I thought his leg was permanently injured. It seemed that bad. He got up and said in his heavy French accent, 'I teenk I cahn plaie.' Salaun then got fifteen out of the next sixteen points and beat me easily in the fourth and fifth games."

No matter how successful you are at controlling your mind, there will be bad days and momentary lapses during a match. "On some days," says Goldie Edwards, "I feel more aggressive than others. I assert myself, get out front and take the upper hand, and cream the ball. On those days, it's important and easy. On other days, I don't have the energy, I just don't care. I nip about at the back and fiddle around.

"If it is a big match and I feel myself slipping, I try to think thoughts of how important it is. I try to relax. I take a deep breath and just let my muscles go, to untense. When receiving the serve, I try to keep a firm grip but a loose arm. A tight arm moves more slowly.

"I try to create a positive feeling that I can do it. I recall previous wins over this same opponent, and over better opponents. There have been times when I thought, 'Well, too bad, this one is gone,' then I relaxed and ended up winning. I was down love-two in the Canadian Open against Jane Dixon, in 1970. Somebody came down and said, 'What you need to do is hit higher shots that break off the walls and keep her going to the back. I did and it worked. I came back and won the next three games. When you're in the heat of a match, it's hard to see everything that is happening. Having the ability to do that for yourself would be marvelous."

At the top levels of the game, players are known for

their abilities to block out everything that doesn't bear on winning. Vic Niederhoffer has a remarkable view of mental control: "I've never had a problem controlling myself. The sport is supposed to be an expression of your personality and your values. By allowing your values to be upset on the court, you are just losing your dignity and becoming less of a person *on* the court than you are *off* the court.

"There is certainly no reason for you to get out of control in the court more than is appropriate in life itself. You should have a general feeling that you are going to concentrate on two or three different things during the game—the ways you can win points and how you should vary the risks that you take during the game. That's probably the thing that you should change the most: how fast you want to end the points, and what type of shots you think are worthy of risk."

The Serve as an Offensive Weapon

Squash is a delicate offensive/defensive ballet, mainly due to its shared-court nature. If one player is hitting slightly offensive shots, the other player is usually countering with slightly defensive shots. Or, at the extremes, one player is making "impossible gets" of the other's "sure winners."

Among advanced players, this principle of offensive/defensive balance is sustained over longer points. At lower levels of play, it is crucial at the beginning of each point—with the serve. And yet, the serve is probably the most neglected part of the game. Perhaps this is so because practicing a squash serve is an awfully boring exercise.

151

Many players use the serve only to put the ball in play. This is a big mistake. It is your first opportunity to hit an offensive shot. If you can take the offense with the serve, then you are on top of the point from the very beginning. But if your serve is just a point starter, or worse, if you lay up a fat ball, someone with a good return of serve will get the first offensive shot. And this may set the tone for the entire point. It could end the point right there.

The Constable Dead-Lob Serve

Betty Constable teaches her women players a high, arching "dead-lob" serve often worth several points a game.

"I crouch low to the floor, with my racquet down low. When I come up through that ball, I don't hit it. I keep it on my racquet as long as possible.

"The racquet contacts the ball with as little speed as possible. I try to soften the blow by putting my whole body into it. Most lob serves are an arm-and-shoulder shot. Not the dead-lob. My arm, shoulder and body all spiral upward together, and I baby it up there. I *ooze* it up there.

"I lean out as far as I can in the forehand court to narrow the angle off the front wall. Since I'm coming through the ball so slowly I can't depend on English.   **153**

"When this serve comes down along the side wall, it's almost as if someone dropped it into the back corner from the ceiling. It's devilishly hard to return, and one of the best ways I have found to beat a man."

Playing to the Score

I have heard that Bob Hetherington, a former Yale star who has held a national ranking for quite a few years, sometimes seals himself off from the score in a match by playing up to 175 isolated points, which is the aggregate of a five-game match in which the score in each game goes to 18-17. He thus cancels out the condition of being ahead or behind, which in turn makes it impossible for the score to have any effect on the quality of his play during a given point. It is said that he sometimes has to be told when the match is over.

Of course, Hetheringtonlike powers of concentration, which are known to be awesome, have not been generally bestowed, so that most players have developed playing habits based on the score. Are they well ahead? Are they behind 10-2 in the third? Is it 13-all in the fifth? What do they do in these situations?

Playing to the score seems to vary a great deal with individual players. For example, I asked Cal Mac-Cracken whether he played conservatively or adventure-somely if he was leading by a large margin. He said, "Never change a winning game. To show you what can happen, I had an experience in 1948, when I was first starting to break into the national scene. I was playing Charlie Brinton, four-time winner of the national championships, and still defending champion, in the quarter-finals of the nationals at the Harvard Club in Boston. I won the first two games fairly easily, like ten and nine, and then in the third game, I had him 14-7, and believe it or not, I lost that game!

"Andy Ingraham spoke to me in the locker room before the fourth game. He said, 'Cal, don't change your game. Keep it exactly the way it was in the first, second, and beginning of the third game. You got panicky trying for that last point and changed it all around. Go back in there and play your standard game.' I did, and I won it about 15-10. So I beat the national champ. That was my first real important victory."

Goldie Edwards, on the other hand, if she is ahead by a large margin, will sometimes play a little bit of cat-and-mouse with her opponent. "I guess it's really a bad thing," she said, "if winning is the only criterion. But I like to have fun, so I play to see how much I can make them run. I get tremendous satisfaction in putting the ball exactly where I want to put it. So I will do lobs and drops just to keep it in play, just for the sake of keeping the point going. And I must admit I do that sometimes when I should be paying more attention to winning the point as soon as I can."

One approach to the score if you are, say, ahead 2-1, it's the fourth game, and you get down by 10-3, is to save yourself for the last game. Certainly you wouldn't try desperately to get balls and risk tiring yourself. You could even try some ridiculous shots that you would not ordinarily attempt in a match. And, with the pressure off temporarily, you might make a few of them. If you don't it doesn't matter. But if you do, it can rattle your opponent, which could be just what you need to make a good start in the fifth game.

On choosing set points to break a tie game, there seems to be more agreement. The better player, the player who is stronger, should choose the greater number of points. The player who is the underdog, who is more tired, and can win only by luck or chance, should choose "no set." An exception to this might occur if your opponent had run five or six points to catch you at 14-all. You might in that case take advantage of a possible temporary letup and force them to play yet another game point.

Momentum is a big factor in squash, perhaps more so than in other racquet sports, because you are given less time and space to compose yourself and dredge up from a slump. As Cal notes, "I think things go in streaks. They certainly do for me." The same is true for Goldie: "I find that if my shots are on, I have great confidence in them, and I play them, and then I'll win a round of points. But as soon as I get nervous and tighten up, or lose confidence in my shots, then it's gone."

Gaining perspective on the score is a good way to shore up your game if things are running against you. It can also be useful so that you don't get carried away with your own prowess and fall into a pit of neglect. Goldie has an interesting way of keeping her head about the score toward the end of a game: "At 12-9 or 9-12, I think of it immediately as being a 3-3 game. You know, three points will finish it off, or three points will tie it. I tend to think of this at 8-12, 9-12, 10-13, all in around there. So if I'm up to 12-8, that's a 3-4 situation. That point doesn't pass me, especially if it's 9-12 or closer, without my thinking about it. In fact, sometimes I've even been tempted to say to my opponent, 'Okay now, that's a 3-3 situation,' but I don't."

Correct Responses to the Basic Shots

"One of the best ways a player can become remarkably better in a short period of time," says Norm Peck, "is to study, practice, and use during play the most effective responses to the basic squash shots.

"The player who uses the correct responses to the basic shots will force opponents more often into difficult hitting positions, will be able to anticipate the shots of better opponents, and will get more pleasure out of the game as a result of intelligent shot choices.

"So let's go through the five basic shots and see what the better responses are for each."

The Rail Shot

Besides the two major options to a rail shot—another rail or a cross-court—a third is the three-wall (Figure **159**

19A). It's not as hard as it looks to a beginner, and it will occasionally nick for a winner (practice will enable you to hit for the nick). The three-wall shot is most effectively hit when the ball is moving almost parallel to and about 6 to 12 inches away from the side wall.

A fourth option to the rail shot is what I call a "sloppy cross-court" (Figure 19B). You can get it to look like the three-wall in the beginning stages, thereby pulling your opponent *toward* the front wall as you hit it. Instead,

Figure 19A

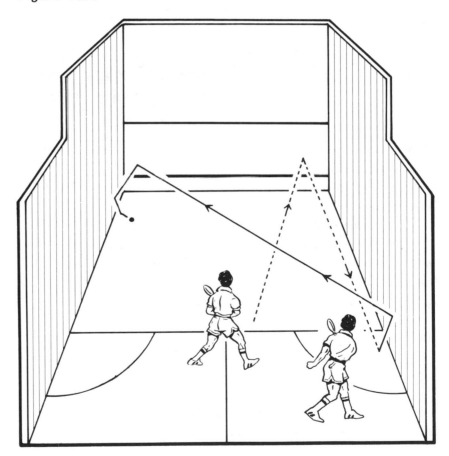

widen the angle and *lift* the ball higher onto the front wall. It will then angle back to the other side wall near the service box.

The "sloppy cross-court" is also a fairly *safe* way of getting a difficult rail shot out of the back court. You are hitting *up* and have no chance at all to hit the tin, which is great from the back court. It's a good shot to keep your opponent deep, thereby increasing the effectiveness of the three-wall when you do choose to use it.

Figure 19B

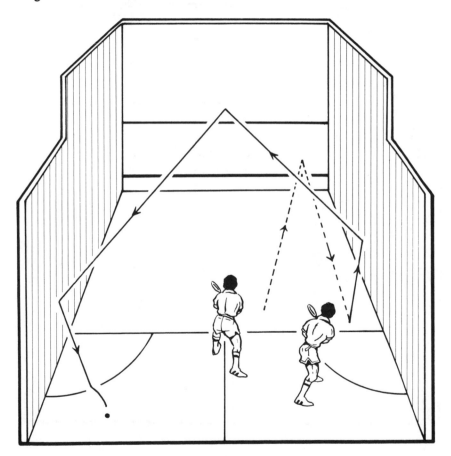

The Cross-Court

If your opponent hits a cross-court that is going to break off the side wall at about the service line, you have three good choices. One (Figure 20A) is to move forward, intercept (volley) the ball *before* it gets to the side wall, and hit a rail shot.

Figure 20A

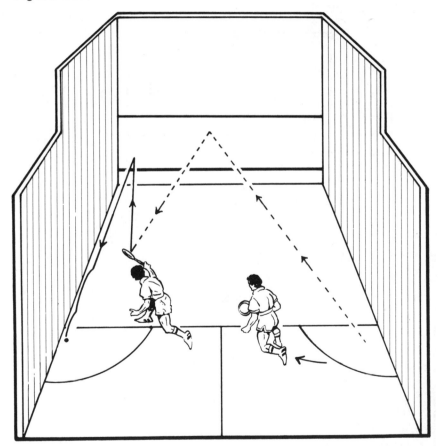

If you cannot intercept your opponent's cross-court, you would have to move back and take it as it breaks off the side wall. In this amount of time the other player would have probably reached the T, so your shot, if possible, should be a cross-court return to the area he or she has vacated (Figure 20B). This is an easy shot to tin, especially if your opponent's shot had good depth and speed. It is important to meet the shot well in front of your body

Figure 20B

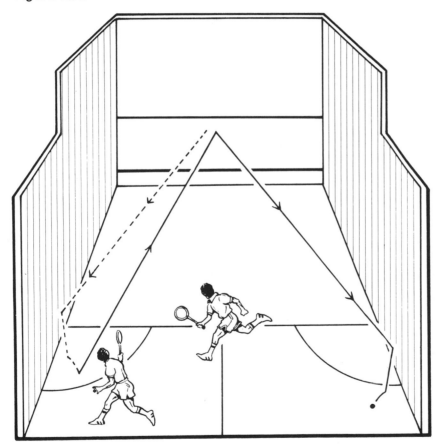

and to stroke the ball, getting good depth and width on the cross-court return.

Your third choice, if you cannot hit a strong cross-court return, is to make a defensive rail shot with emphasis on gluing it to the wall (Figure 20C). You can make this a kind of half lob as long as you keep it tight to the wall. On this shot you are hitting for position, so that you can get back on the T and stay in the point.

Figure 20C

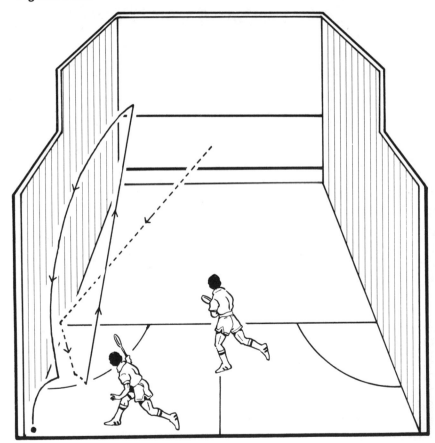

The Reverse Corner

Your opponent, after hitting a reverse corner, has to step through the ball to avoid a let situation. So as he or she pulls through the ball, you move up to intercept the shot (Figure 21A).

If you meet the ball early enough, and you're fairly

Figure 21A

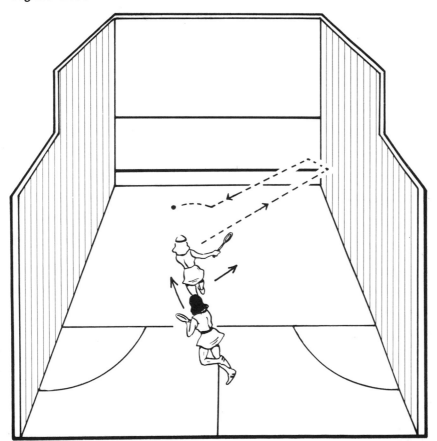

close to the front wall, you should hit a drop shot. It should die before it hits the side wall (Figure 21B).

If you get to the ball a little slower, and it's also a little farther back from the front wall, then you will probably

Figure 21B

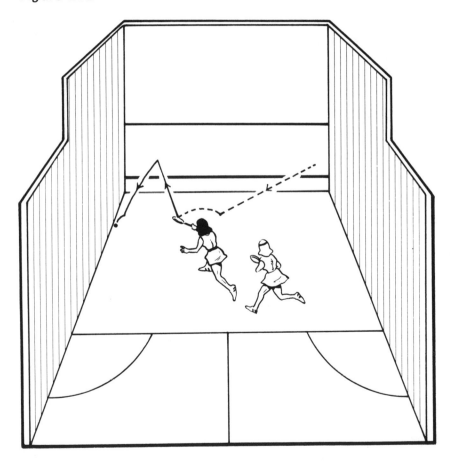

feel more comfortable hitting a rail shot. And it doesn't have to be a low, hard rail shot. It just has to reach the service box on the first bounce and not come off the side wall (Figure 21C).

Figure 21C

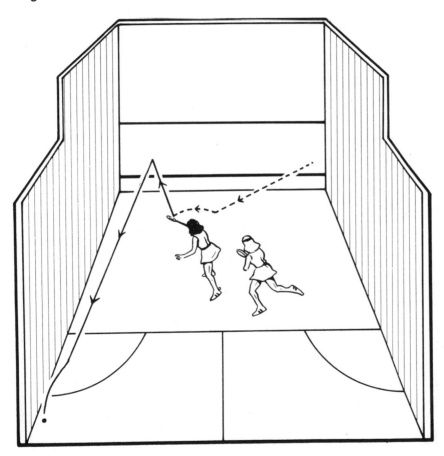

The Reverse Corner—Weak Response

Many players when drawn up to the front court by a reverse corner will panic. For example (Figure 22A), they rush up, usually arriving just in time to scrape the ball off the floor, get a glaze over their eyes, and just hit. And be-

Figure 22A

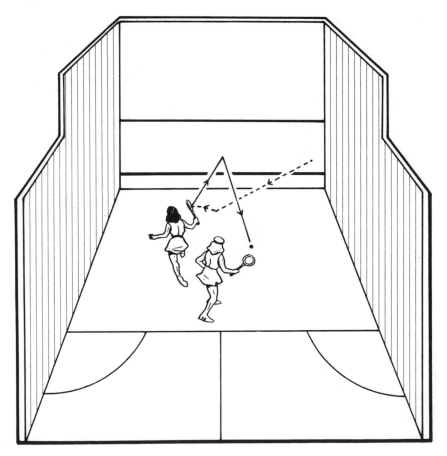

cause they have arrived facing the front wall, the shot they hit is a cross-court, right back to their opponent!

Two other less desirable returns of the reverse corner are both cross-the-body shots resulting also from facing the front wall. The first (Figure 22B) is a forehand reverse corner to the left which goes right back to your

Figure 22B

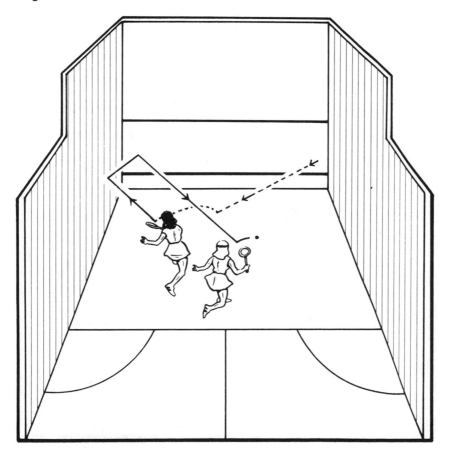

opponent. The second (Figure 22C) is a backhand reverse corner to the right, fairly effective in terms of positioning, but tremendously difficult to hit.

The Roll Corner

The roll corner (Figure 23) is hit by your opponent as a change of pace when you are expecting a rail shot. If hit

Figure 22C

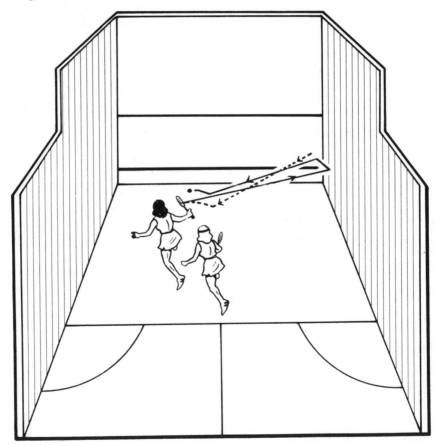

correctly it will bounce twice before it reaches the third wall. If the shot is poorly timed or executed and you get your racquet on it, you have two good choices of return. If the other player is moving toward the front wall, you should hit a rail (1). If the player remains further back, which usually happens, your best shot would be a straight drop (2).

Figure 23

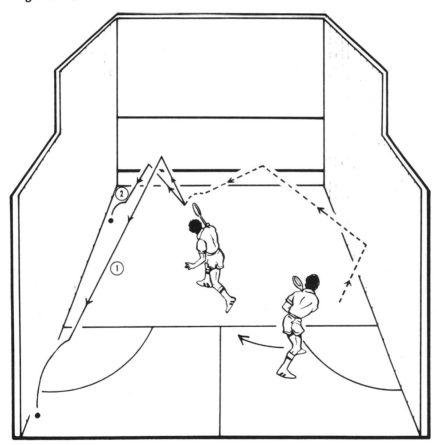

The Three-Wall Shot

The correct positioning to return a three-wall shot (Figure 24) is to play it with your *back*hand if it is on your *back*hand side, and vice versa. This way you are in a better position to hit a ball coming *toward* you instead of *across* your body. You are also in a *much* better position to *disguise* your shot. The two best choices in this case are a drop (1) or rail shot (2).

Figure 24

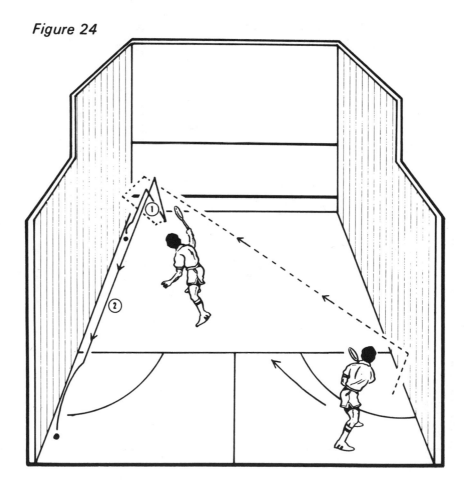

The Three-Wall Shot—Weak Response

Most three-wall shots are not hit well enough to nick. They usually sit up, giving you enough time to reach them. And yet many players give up when they see that shot heading for the opposite corner. Or, if they do go up and retrieve the shot, as in Figure 25, they approach the shot from the wrong side, which forces an incorrect response that returns the ball to their opponent.

Figure 25

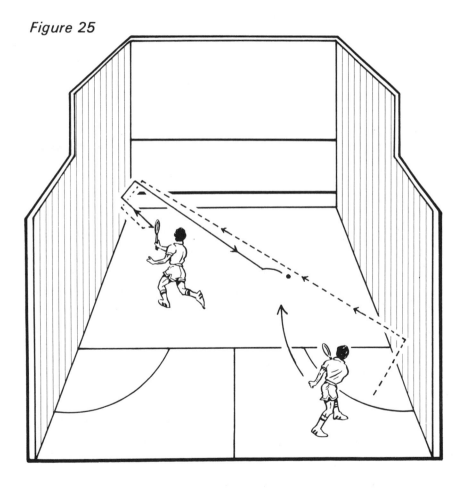

Shot Zones

As one who often shoots without thinking, I have wondered over the possibility of a mental crutch which would force me to select the correct shot in most situations. How often do you line up on the ball and, with plenty of time to select the best shot, end up by hitting an angled number which goes right back to your opponent's cocked racquet?

Shot selection can be reduced to a certain number of basics which, if followed, would bring considerable improvement to the games of most players at the intermediate level.

This boiling down of shots into an instant strategy, as it were, I have called "shot zones." The concept is that if

you are standing in one of these zones, you hit the indicated shot. You will of course give up the refinement of choice typically made by top-level players, but the hope is that by doing so you will avoid a far greater number of shot-selection blunders.

These shot zones depend on what ball is being used, so in Figure 26 I have devised two zone diagrams, one for the 70+ ball (A) and one for the West Company Blue Dot (B). The reason that there is no lob up front with the 70+ ball is that the ball has to be hit too high onto the front wall to make the lob a practical shot for mid-level players from that zone. In both diagrams, the short shot from the T assumes that your opponent is behind you.

Figure 26A. 70+   *Figure 26B. Blue Dot*

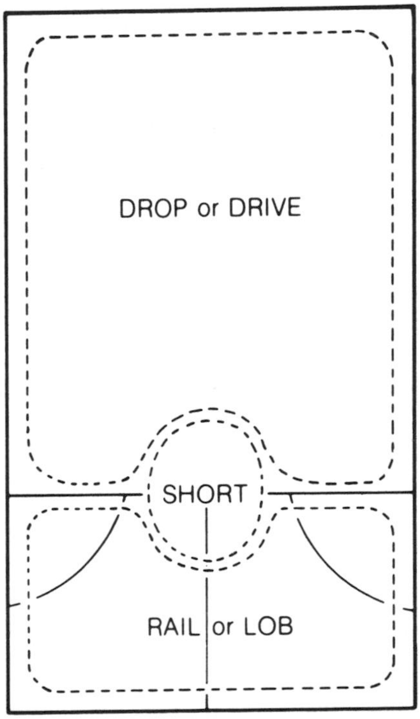

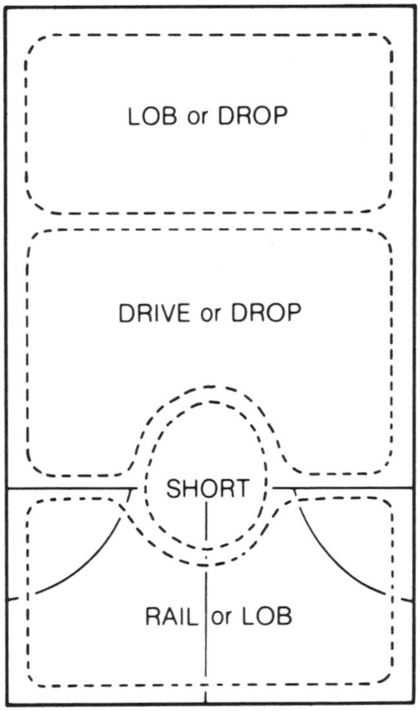

DROP or DRIVE

SHORT

RAIL or LOB

LOB or DROP

DRIVE or DROP

SHORT

RAIL or LOB

The drive indicated is either a rail or a cross-court drive. The lobs should generally be kept along the walls as opposed to cross-court lobs. The only time an angled shot other than the cross-court drive should be used is from the T, where a reverse corner or roll corner is permissible. Giving up these beautiful angles will pain some players, but then of course that is the whole idea.

Deception *Is the Essence of Squash*

Of all the racquet games, squash is the trickiest. Many points end with an opponent scurrying *away* from where the ball has actually been aimed. Deception won the point. It follows therefore that squash is the most challenging mentally of all racquet sports. Some would go even further and say of all physical contests.

Cal MacCracken, who plays a lot of tennis and squash, says, "The biggest difference to me is that in squash *deception* is an *extremely* important part of the game. You have to learn to hit your five basic shots with the view from your rear end looking the same. That you learn by *yourself* in playing alone in a court and rallying. You make *sure* that you hit all of your shots with your feet the same way.

177

"When you don't play a great deal, you begin to give clues as to what shot you're hitting, and you no longer have the element of surprise on your side. Your opponent knows what you're doing. An observant opponent watches you all of the time and knows what shot you're getting ready to hit. You signal this with your feet, racquet, hands, and body.

"The great players I have played against tried to deceive me in every way as to the shot they were going to hit. A typical example of that was Jack Summers, pro at M.I.T., who was national professional champion (and whose son Bill later became the coach at Princeton). I used to watch him play Sherman Howes from Boston. Howes was a tremendous power hitter. He could hit the ball so hard you'd think it was going right through the wall. Howes was champion of the Boston area at that time. He'd come up to Summers, who was twenty-five or thirty years older than he was, and he'd say, 'Five dollars on this game.' So they'd play and Howes would win, and then he'd win the second game and Summers would be down ten bucks. Then Summers would say, 'Double or nothing on this,' and would win the next three in a row with the most amazing deceptions. Howes would just stand there thinking the ball was going one way and it would go the other.

"All things being equal, and maybe even when they're a little unequal, I'd put my money on a deceptive player every time."

Coping with
a Wild Swinger

Occasionally, at the nether levels of league play, one encounters the super athlete who is new to squash. You know the type: superb physique, hard-hitting shots when the racquet happens to meet the ball, but one hell of an overswing. More like a windmill than anything remotely resembling a squash player. What do you do if you don't want to have your head taken off and also don't want to forfeit the match? Cal MacCracken has some good advice for coping with a wild swinger.

"If the guy is making great motions with his racquet, then he isn't making many with his feet. Therefore he is probably not quick afoot. And he's probably leaving a lot of court unprotected, such as up front. I would use a lot of drop shots. He does have an advantage in the back of the **179** court, where he is swinging around making you duck out of the way. So I would not give him shots in the back of the court. I would hit every shot as a straight drop, or a cross-court drop, or a reverse corner or a roll corner, and make him spend all of his time rushing up front. You let him take shots in the back court and his windmill becomes his strength."

Vic Niederhoffer has a similar view: "Wild swingers tend to be a little bit erratic in their play. And they're not too good when they're forced to move. So the idea is to hit the ball as far away from them as possible. Try not to keep the ball down the walls, but hit a lot of cross-courts."

The 50-mph Rail Shot

A handful of world-class players can drive a rail shot from about 1 foot above the tin without a bounce to a rear-wall nick. Such a shot would travel on a hard, flat trajectory to its target at over 100 miles per hour. These same players more often hit a breadwinning rail shot a few inches over the tin at, say, 70 mph, which bounces once at the service line and again right at the rear wall. (Figure 27A). This is the classic hard, low rail, tight to the wall, that any player would love to own.

Indeed, how many intermediate and lesser players do you know who try to blast the ball just above the tin and down the rail only to have it tee up at about the service line for a putaway (Figure 27B)? What they are doing is trading control (and points) for power. What they should do is learn to hit the "50-mph rail shot" (Figure 27A). **181**

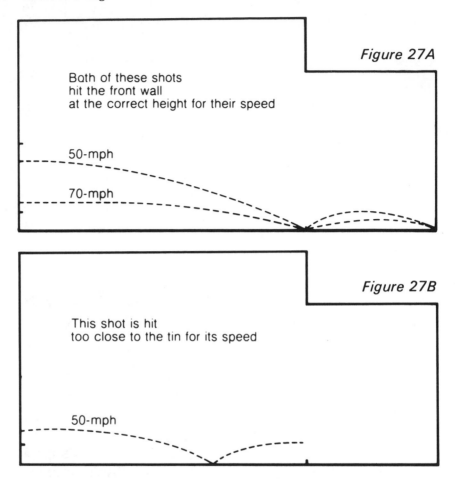

Figure 27A

Both of these shots
hit the front wall
at the correct height for their speed

50-mph

70-mph

Figure 27B

This shot is hit
too close to the tin for its speed

50-mph

The speed will vary with court temperatures, the type of ball and the player's skill, but the concept is simple: less than top-level players should avoid the dynamite rail shot in favor of one slow enough to hit safely, time after time, close along the wall and deep to the rear corner. This shot will win points regardless of its speed.

Mastering the 50-mph rail shot is also a fine way of reckoning with your own abilities and playing consistently up to your potential.

Four Shots
by Niederhoffer

"I've pioneered four things in the game.

"One is using the three-wall nick as the most important shot in the game. You can hit it so that it makes a winner, and very rarely will it make a loser. There's a comfortable, big margin above the tin.

"I've also used a cross-court drop shot very effectively. I think almost all the players are now beginning to use that.

"Then there is the hard, criss-cross serve on every point. That's something I've pioneered. It should still be good with the Seventy-plus ball.

"Then there is this new thing I've come up with, which is bouncing the ball before I serve a high, reverse-corner **183** serve (Figure 28). I do this on the backhand also. You have to get around behind the ball. I've played whole games using nothing but this serve. I've won a lot of matches with it. I worked on it three times a week for six weeks about eight months ago. Many players have used that serve toward the end of a match from time to time as a humorous thing, but I was the first one to employ it as a

Figure 28. Niederhoffer's Bounce Reverse-Corner Serve

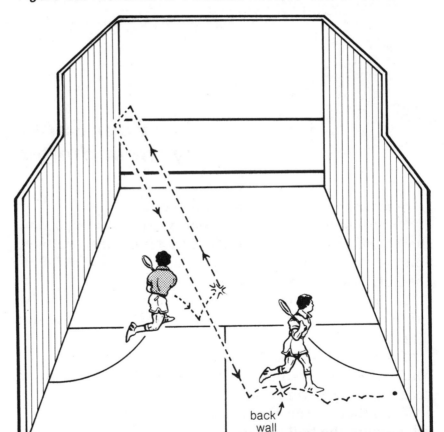

back
wall

major offensive weapon. It's very effective. The beauty of it is that if it bounces on the floor, there's almost no way to return it. It has to be volleyed. If you could really master it, and I haven't yet, you could win an enormous number of points with it."

Hot Court, Cold Court?

Goldie Edwards always thought squash was played in hot courts until she came to Pretty Brook Club in Princeton, N.J., to play in the New Jersey State Open. "Our courts in Pittsburgh are above the wrestling rooms at the University. They are marvelous courts, but hot air rises so the ball goes around like a mad thing. When I came to Pretty Brook, it was zero degrees out, and the front wall of the court is the wall of the building. The wall was dead. The ball didn't bounce. It was like a piece of concrete. I had one of those Fred Perry skirts with green trim and a green sweater to match. They told me to take off my green sweater, the tournament was all whites. I didn't know that. I was freezing. It was so cold my hands were white." Goldie didn't win. It was her first women's tournament. But as she said, "It was a beginning."

The distinction between hot-court and cold-court squash is one that a lot of players don't understand, according to Cal MacCracken. "New York City is full of a lot of hot courts. The ball gets very bouncy as the game progresses and yet you go out into the suburbs and play in icy-cold courts. So there are two different games. A lot of the players would win at one game and get beaten at the other because they couldn't adjust to the other type of court.

"I think one of my strong points was that I was able to adapt to those conditions and switch my game. The key in hot-court squash is to change the angle at which you hit the ball. In hot courts you want the ball to come off the *side* wall *before* it hits the floor. Your drives have to be at a wider angle cross-court. If you can hit them hard, hit them a little deeper and hit them coming off the side wall every time, you can force the other person into errors. That plus the three-wall nick are things that win for you in hot-court squash.

"The old Princeton Club courts on Thirty-ninth Street and Park Avenue were very hot. A couple of them were even squash tennis courts, *narrower* than regulation, so you *had* to know how to do that, and I learned that trick pretty well.

"On the other hand, when you get into *cold* courts you get into straight drops, reverse corners, and roll corners. These shots will just die up front in a cold court, but they won't do you nearly as much good in a hot court."

Parting Shots

Here are a few items I collected while researching this book which fit nowhere in particular but are too good to leave out.

The Importance of Positioning. It is much easier to learn the shots than it is to get in position to make them. Once you are in position, the stroke is always the same, but getting there can take a thousand variations. If you are out of position, you can have the best forehand in town and it won't do you any good.

Backing on the Ball. Betty Constable gives this advice to get you in position to hit a ball that has angled off the side wall and is being hit off the rear wall: "You never move back and stop and freeze your feet to the floor. By doing that you've committed yourself. You should always be moving so that at the last minute you step back into the ball. This way you hit it while you're moving forward and everything comes down at once. Your foot comes down and your racquet comes down to hit the ball.

"To get a ball like that, the moment you know it is going to come around and off the back wall, you should follow the ball with your racquet, like a pointer. It's a smooth, rhythmic way of getting your racquet back."

Watching Your Opponent. When watching your opponent behind you, keep your feet well spread and parallel to the front wall. Turn *only* the top part of your body to watch. That way you can push off in either direction to retrieve a shot. Two common errors made in this situation are turning your feet toward your opponent, which prevents you from getting around quick enough for a cross-court shot, and having your feet together, which keeps you from being able to push off quickly in any direction.

Using Video Tape. We use video tape at the Princeton Club of New York to instruct at all levels. There is no way to duplicate its instant replay and stop-action capability through other teaching alternatives. The mental images thus conveyed of one's own strokes and court mannerisms are a valuable input for use in mental practice as well as on-court practice.

Cal MacCracken was exposed to video a few years ago. This is what he has to say about it: "Bill Summers had a video machine in the gallery at Princeton's squash courts and he was video taping all of his players. He asked me if I wanted to do it. So I went in and played with one of his varsity players there and came up afterwards to look at it, and I got the shock of my life. I said, 'Is that me?' I thought I was running around with my knees bent as I should, but instead I was absolutely stiff-legged. I was wondering why I was so slow, and that was the reason. I would never have realized this without video."

A Match Checklist. If you are not accustomed to getting ready for an important match, it would be a good idea to go through a checklist and countdown process starting a few days before your match, as follows:

1. *Equipment:* Is my grip okay? Does it need a new wrap? Strings in good shape? Second racquet okay? Do I have a change of squash clothes if required to play several rounds or more at an away tournament?

2. *Conditioning:* Taper off from strenuous exercise about forty-eight hours ahead. Last hard match should leave two days rest. Play and shot practice okay one day ahead but no marathons.

3. *Intake:* A match diet is discussed under "What to Eat Before a Match." The only thing to add here would be to advise you to eat normally for an athlete prior to a match, and to arrive for play with neither too full nor too empty a stomach.

4. *Last few hours before match time:* Depending on your age and daily routine, you should have the right amount of relaxation and quiet time to prepare your head and body for maximum performance. Vic Niederhoffer relaxes before play, "mainly because the body's getting old and it needs some rest." He lies down, especially with two matches in a day and tries not to do anything hard with the eyes, like reading or watching TV.

5. *Muscle state:* Are your muscles loose, relaxed, and warm? A half hour before match time, do the stretching exercises described under "A Program for Squash Muscles," and warm up sufficiently to raise

the internal heat of your muscles and get the joints well lubricated with sinovial fluid.

6. *Alertness:* Are you awake? You can't focus your eyes if you aren't completely awake. If it is not the right time of day for your normal peak performance, an extra bit of warm-up will help you wake up. Cold water on the face and washing out your mouth helps too.

Play Within Your Limits. You can have the greatest strategy in the world, but if you can't execute that strategy, you are hopeless in having conceived it. "The 50-mph Rail Shot" and "Shot Zones," among other sections of this book, are intended to help mid-level players realize their potential, given their limitations and capabilities.

So You Think Your Opponent Is Tired? Squash opponents are like salmon. Once they are tired, if you don't keep working them, you're going to rest them and lose them (the match). More times than I care to admit, I have had opponents heaving and glazed after a long rally and considered that I only had to keep the ball in play to have them utterly collapse in exhaustion. The fallacy in this plan is that you stop applying the pressure which produced the desired effect in the first place and you begin relaxing, only to realize, too late, that the tables have turned.

Fair Play. What do you do if your opponent keeps playing shots after the second bounce? Vic Niederhoffer has an approach to this which I like. "You have to realize that if you want to be a good sport, it's a personal thing. You shouldn't worry about your opponent. That's his business. To hold a grudge because the other person is cheating and you're not is really not very mature.

"Tell your opponent he's hitting them on two bounces.

The main thing to understand is that very often your opponent doesn't realize the ball has bounced twice. You have to be pretty good to really know what you're doing wrong in this game. Most players, when they are told they got it on two bounces, will be pleased to play the point over. Which is the fair thing to do. The worst thing to do is dwell on it with an envious feeling that they're getting away with something that you're not getting away with.

"If that doesn't work, ask for a referee, and if you go that way, then neither of you calls anything on yourself. Let the referee make all the decisions."

Being Prepared. Again, Professor Niederhoffer: "If there is any key to winning, it lies in preparation. Preparation comes many months before your match, when you're running around the track or practicing hundreds of three-wall nicks. If you're not tired and you're in an equilibrium position where you are strong near the end, then you can hit shots offensively rather than defensively, and develop your game within a more competitive framework. You will have more respect for your own abilities to keep going. You will be more resilient in defeat, and more worthy in victory."